# 100

## THINGS TO DO IN
## ALABAMA
## BEFORE YOU
## DIE

# 100

## THINGS TO DO IN ALABAMA BEFORE YOU DIE

· · · · · · · · · · · · · · · · · · · · · · · ·

## MARY JOHNS WILSON

REEDY PRESS

Library of Congress Control Number: 2019938582

ISBN: 9781681062365

Design by Jill Halpin

All photos provided by the author unless otherwise noted.

Printed in the United States of America
19 20 21 22 23    5 4 3 2 1

Please note that websites, phone numbers, addresses, and company names are subject to change or cancellation. We did our best to relay the most accurate information available, but due to circumstances beyond our control, please do not hold us liable for misinformation. When exploring new destinations, please do your homework before you go.

# DEDICATION

To Matt for believing in me and making travel across Alabama so much fun.

# CONTENTS

● ● ● ● ● ● ● ● ● ● ● ● ● ● ● ● ● ● ● ● ● ● ● ●

## Music and Entertainment

• • • • • • • • • • • • • • • • • • • • • • • • • • • • • •

**Sports and Recreation**

• • • • • • • • • • • • • • • • • • • • • • • • • • • • • • •

## Culture and History

• • • • • • • • • • • • • • • • • • • • • • • • • • • •

. . . . . . . . . . . . . . . . . . . . . . . . . . . .

# PREFACE

When I was a child growing up in rural Kentucky, daring to utter the words "I'm bored" in front of adults was a surefire way to earn a list of chores as boredom's cure. I quickly learned that a preferable alternative to whining was to simply go exploring, whether that was a hike down through the creek or a bike ride into town to visit friends.

As an adult, I still enjoy going on adventures to find new treasures in big cities and hidden gems in tiny towns. Here, I share one hundred ideas for experiencing the best my new home state has to offer—from mountains to beaches, barbecue to fine dining, the Civil War to civil rights, and metropolitan museums to agritourism attractions. So the next time you're bored, don't whine. Pick up this book, choose a page, and head out to create your own adventure!

*Photo courtesy Matt Wilson*

# ACKNOWLEDGMENTS

This book would not be possible without my sister, Audra Meighan. Your ability to support your loved ones and help people make dreams into realities is unsurpassed. Thanks to my parents, who instilled in me a love for exploring country roads, and thanks to my coworkers at Simply Southern TV and the Alabama Farmers Federation. It is a joy to work with you on finding and sharing the good stories about the great state of Alabama.

*Photo courtesy Caleb Hicks*

# FOOD AND DRINK

# SMOTHER BARBECUE CHICKEN IN WHITE SAUCE
## AT BIG BOB GIBSON BAR-B-Q

North Carolina has its signature vinegar-based barbecue sauce, while Kansas City–style barbecue lovers prefer a thick, tomato-based sauce. Thanks to Big Bob Gibson, Alabama has its own regional barbecue sauce. Gibson's trademark tangy white sauce uses mayonnaise as its base mixed with enough black pepper to give it a good bite.

A former railroad worker and a giant of a man, Gibson started serving his white sauce poured over barbecue chicken or pork back in 1925. Today, the fourth generation of the Gibson family carries on Big Bob's tradition with two restaurants in Decatur. Diners enjoy a greater selection of menu items now, including smoked turkey, ribs, barbecue baked potatoes, and barbecue salads. For those who prefer a red sauce, the family developed its own recipe in 1997, which is a two-time winner of the Memphis in May World Championship Barbecue Cooking Contest. To try both sauces along with the restaurant's award-winning smoked meats, order the Big Bob Gibson Combo with St. Louis cut spare ribs, pulled pork, and a quarter chicken.

1715 Sixth Ave. SE, Decatur, AL 35601
(256) 350-6969

2520 Danville Rd. SW, Decatur, AL 35603
(256) 350-0404

BigBobGibson.com

# SMELL WHAT'S COOKING
## AT CONECUH SAUSAGE

An unmistakable aroma wafts by cars and trucks as they're driven down Interstate 65 through Conecuh County in Southwest Alabama. It's that succulent smell of hickory-smoked sausage. Located just off Exit 96, the Conecuh Sausage Company's forty-two-thousand-square-foot plant produces between thirty thousand and forty thousand pounds of spicy, savory Conecuh Sausage every day.

Owned and operated by the Sessions family since 1947, the business now offers six kinds of sausage, including a no-MSG variety, along with smoked hams, smoked turkeys, smoked bacon, hot dogs, and seasonings. Motorists who follow their noses can find all Conecuh Sausage has to offer at the gift shop the family built in front of the plant. If you have to try before you buy, the shop offers free samples, and suffice it to say, once you try it, your salivating taste buds won't be satisfied with just a sample.

200 Industrial Park, Evergreen, AL 36401
(251) 578-3380, ConecuhSausage.com

# STOP BY JESSE'S RESTAURANT AFTER A DRIVE
## THROUGH MAGNOLIA SPRINGS

If the gold-paved roads of heaven aren't shaded with live oaks, I'm not sure I want to go. Instead, I'll stay in Magnolia Springs, a little town dripping with Southern charm. True to the town's name, magnolia trees are prevalent in this precious hamlet, as are dogwoods, camellias, wisteria vines, and azaleas. Built on the Magnolia River, past residents traveled the area by sailboat or paddleboat, and mail is still delivered by boat.

A stop in Magnolia Springs isn't complete until you've enjoyed a first-class meal at Jesse's Restaurant, a casual, fine-dining establishment. Opened in 1999 in a building that once housed the Moore Bros. Store, the eatery is named for the old storekeeper, Jesse King. The chef at Jesse's is dedicated to using local products, especially seafood. Start with the seasonal boutique oysters, especially if they're from Bayou La Batre or Murder Point. Keep the local seafood trend going with the Gulf shrimp and grits or venture back to the turf with a King's Cut bone-in filet.

14770 Oak St., Magnolia Springs, AL 36555
(251) 965-3827, JessesRestaurant.com

# TEAR INTO FRIED CHICKEN
## AT THE CHICKEN SHACK

Southerners want our tea sweet, our peas black-eyed, and our chicken fried, and in Alabama no one fries up chicken better than the folks at the Chicken Shack in Luverne. Cooks at the Chicken Shack have used the same recipe for frying chicken since the establishment opened in 1968. Their secret to success is a salt-based marinade with a crunchy, light breading, which earned the restaurant the title of Bama's Best Fried Chicken in a 2018 contest.

The popular poultry purveyors fry up more than two thousand pounds of chicken every week, and in a town of less than three thousand people, that's more than 1.5 pounds of chicken per citizen. Of course, it's not just the locals who eat at the Chicken Shack. Its prime location off Highway 331 makes it a favorite pit stop for beachbound travelers. For those in a hurry, you can call in an order and pick it up from the walk-up window, but there's also a spacious dining room for diners who want to put their feet up and sit a spell.

665 Forest Ave., Luverne, AL 36049
(334) 335-6566, facebook.com/The-Chicken-Shack-202523113230813

# GRAB A SLICE OF PECAN PIE
## AT PRIESTER'S

The Priester's Pecans store in Fort Deposit serves as a sweet pit stop smack-dab in the middle of a road trip down Interstate 65. While there's plenty of store merchandise to peruse, pecan candies are the stars of the show. In fact, you can watch from the second-floor observation area as workers create pecan-laden confections that are a treat to the taste buds and the olfactory senses.

With plenty of free samples in the store, try all the creatively flavored pecans—from Key lime and praline to cinnamon and honey-glazed. Family owned and operated since 1935, the Priester's still finds new ways to dress up and serve pecans, and it has ample supply, as Alabama ranks sixth in the United States for pecan production.

If you buy only one thing on your visit to Priester's, though, make it the pecan pie. It's the perfect amount of sweet with a crust that flakes so perfectly that your grandmother will wish she had the recipe.

80 Bishop Bottom Rd., Fort Deposit, AL 36032
(334) 227-8355, priesters.com

# CATCH A THROWED ROLL
## AT LAMBERT'S CAFE

Look alive! A meal at Lambert's Cafe is never dull, with warm, yeasty rolls whizzing past patrons. Throwing rolls started at the original Lambert's location in Sikeston, Missouri. On a busy day, as the owner struggled to move through the packed restaurant with hot rolls, a hungry patron suggested he simply throw the baked good. The suggestion took hold and spread to more places when Lambert's opened a second location in Ozark, Missouri, and its third location in Foley, Alabama. You can eat the rolls plain, sopped in sorghum, or smothered with apple butter.

Even though it's just eight miles from the beach, this isn't a seafood joint. Lambert's specializes in true Southern favorites, such as chicken liver or gizzards, a pork chop sandwich, or chicken and dumplings. For sides, waiters bring out bottomless, pass-around buckets of fried okra, black-eyed peas, and other specialties, so you're sure to be as full as a tick by the time you leave.

2981 S. McKenzie, Foley, AL 36535
(251) 943-7655, ThrowedRolls.com

### TIP
Get there early. As a popular beach destination, there's often a line of hungry diners wrapped around the building during prime meal times.

# EAT BAMA'S BEST BURGER
## AT BLACK ROCK BISTRO

Chefs Greg and Lindsey Kilgore met in culinary school in Birmingham and honed their craft in New Orleans restaurants before Hurricane Katrina forced them to evacuate. The couple decided to bring their skills to Greg's hometown of Jasper, which was once one of the world's largest producers of coal. The Kilgores have won over the blue-collar town with their world-class cuisine, and in 2017 they won over the Alabama Cattlemen's Association, winning the group's Bama's Best Burger contest with the Alabama Burger.

The half-pound burger is ground in-house. With such a savory foundation, the typical burger accoutrements of lettuce, onion, and a red tomato just wouldn't suffice. This burger is dressed up with true Southern fixins of pimento cheese, mayonnaise, and a fried-green tomato. Black Rock Bistro also offers tasty Creole and Cajun-inspired dishes, such as catfish Pontchartrain, named one of the "100 Dishes to Eat in Alabama Before You Die" by the Alabama Tourism Department.

313 Nineteenth St. W., Jasper, AL 35501
(205) 387-0282

# DINE
## AT A FIRST-CLASS RESTAURANT

If your culinary picture of Alabama is made up only of BBQ joints and country cooking meat-and-threes, then you're missing out on the state's numerous nationally acclaimed restaurants, led by chefs who balance Southern charm and comfort with sophisticated flair.

The James Beard Awards have been called the "Oscars" for the culinary world. In 2018, Highlands Bar & Grill won the James Beard Award for Most Outstanding Restaurant, while its pastry chef, Dolester Miles, took home the James Beard Award for Most Outstanding Pastry Chef. Owner and executive chef Frank Stitt has a James Beard Award of his own for Best Chef in the Southeast from 2001. Stitt had a great influence on the 2012 James Beard Best Chef in the South, Chris Hastings of Hot & Hot Fish Club. The other chefs listed here have all been semifinalists for the prestigious awards.

**Highlands Bar & Grill and chef Frank Stitt
with pastry chef Dolester Miles**
2011 Eleventh Ave. S., Birmingham, AL 35205
(205) 939-1400, HighlandsBarAndGrill.com

**Hot & Hot Fish Club and chef Chris Hastings**
2180 Eleventh Ct. S., Birmingham, AL 35205
(205) 933-5474, HotAndHotFishClub.com

**Johnny's Restaurant and chef Timothy Hontzas**
2902 Eighteenth St. S., Suite 200, Homewood, AL 35209
(205) 802-2711, JohnnysHomewood.com

**Fisher's Upstairs and chef Bill Briand**
27075 Marina Rd., Orange Beach, AL 36561
(251) 981-7305, FishersOBM.com

**Acre and chef David Bancroft**
210 E. Glenn Ave., Auburn, AL 36830
(334) 246-3763, acreauburn.com

**SpringHouse and chef Rob McDaniel**
12 Benson Mill Rd., Alexander City, AL 35010
(256) 215-7080, SpringhouseAtCrossroads.com

# ENJOY THE SCENERY AND THE SPREAD
## AT RATTLESNAKE SALOON

When visiting a saloon, you expect a taxi ride to come at the end of the night, but at Rattlesnake Saloon the taxi ride comes before your dining experience. In pure Alabama style, patrons climb into the bed of a pickup truck taxi for the drive from the parking lot down to the coolest dive in the state. Literally. Nestled under a craggy, rocky overhang, the Rattlesnake Saloon offers cool air that is a welcome reprieve from sultry Alabama summers.

Built in 2009 as a watering hole for horse trail riders visiting the property, the saloon brings a Wild West feel to the Heart of Dixie. You almost expect to see the Duke himself ride up, tie his trusty steed to the hitching posts, and mosey through the swinging saloon doors. Rattlesnake Saloon is open for lunch and dinner. If you want beer, cider, or wine, stop by after 5:00 p.m. and remember to bring your ID. You don't want to have to hike back up the hill for it.

1292 Mount Mills Rd., Tuscumbia, AL 35674
(256) 370-7220, RattlesnakeSaloon.net

# SAMPLE
# CHOCOLATE GRAVY
## AT STAGGS GROCERY

It sounds wrong, but once you try this Appalachian favorite from Staggs Grocery in Florence, you'll know it is oh-so-right. The rich, chocolate gravy is poured over an open-faced, homemade biscuit and topped with a heaping dollop of butter. The dish is served with crispy bacon, the perfect salty balance to the sweet chocolate. For the biggest appetites, Staggs offers a double order.

Aside from the great taste of a regional oddity, Staggs Grocery is a must-stop for its atmosphere. Patrons place orders directly with the cooks, who also serve as the waitstaff. Seating is family-style, and the locals love to strike up conversations with strangers. When it comes time to pay the bill, the restaurant runs on the honor system. The whole dining experience is reminiscent of simpler times.

Take note—Staggs serves chocolate gravy only on Fridays, but Monday through Thursday you can still enjoy a breakfast or lunch that tastes like something your mawmaw would make.

1424 Huntsville Rd., Florence, AL 35630
(256) 764-7382

# GOBBLE UP A MEAL
## AT BATES HOUSE OF TURKEY

Who says turkey and cornbread dressing smothered in gravy is a meal you can enjoy only once a year? At Bates House of Turkey, you can enjoy all your Thanksgiving favorites no matter what month the calendar reads. The restaurant has been a Greenville establishment since 1970, when the Bates family opened it to promote its farm-raised turkeys. In addition to a full lunch menu featuring turkey sandwiches and a traditional Thanksgiving dinner, the restaurant sells frozen turkeys along with casseroles, soups, and sausages, all made with meat from the turkeys raised at Bates Turkey Farm.

Located in Fort Deposit, just up the road from the restaurant, Bates Turkey Farm started in 1923 when newlywed couple W. C. and Helen Bates received nine turkey eggs as a wedding present. It's been passed down from generation to generation, with the fifth generation of Bates family members now working in the business.

Bates House of Turkey, 1001 Fort Dale Rd., Greenville, AL 36037
(334) 382-6123

Bates Turkey Farm, 45 Bates Rd., Fort Deposit, AL 36032
(888) 249-4505

BatesTurkey.com

# DID YOU KNOW?

Since 1949, the Bates family has provided two turkeys, ceremoniously named Clyde and Henrietta, for Alabama's governor to officially pardon before Thanksgiving.

# SAVOR SEVEN-LAYER CAKES
## FROM DEAN'S CAKE HOUSE

After years working as a cashier at a local grocery store, Dean Jacobs decided it was time she went out on her own. Armed with a lifetime of baking experience, she opened Dean's Cake House in 1994. While the store offers cookies, pies, fudge, brownies, and most other kinds of baked goods your sweet tooth could desire, true to its name, the cakes are the real draw to Ms. Dean's. Thirteen two-layer cake varieties are offered, as well as the store's signature seven-layer cake. Why seven layers? Dean says it's because that's how many layers would fit under the dome of the cake stand.

These cakes taste like something your grandmother would make because, well, Dean is a grandmother, as are the majority of her eighteen employees. Together, the owner and her staff whip up nearly five hundred cakes daily, by hand. If you can't make it down to Andalusia to visit the Cake House itself, you might find Dean's Cakes lurking on store shelves at a local, independent grocer. Find a list of retailers at the Dean's Cake House website.

402 Snowden Dr., Andalusia, AL 36420
(334) 222-0459, DeansCakeHouse.com

# SINK YOUR TEETH
## INTO BISHOP'S BARBECUE

L. O. Bishop is a character with a regional reputation for quippy one-liners. Ask him how he's doing and he'll tell you, "I'm good, but the doctors say it won't last." One of his friends won their hometown Liar's Contest by simply telling the judges, "I rode with L. O. Bishop for three hours, all the way from North Alabama to the beach, and he didn't have a single thing to say."

Turning tales and telling jokes aren't L. O.'s only talents. He's also a skilled BBQ pitmaster for his family's business, Bishop's Barbecue, and he's passed that knowledge on to his son, Luther, the third generation of the family to man the BBQ pit. Every week they smoke 5,200 pounds of Boston butts, low and slow. After about twenty hours over a hickory fire, the pork is pulled and vacuum-sealed in packages weighing one or five pounds and frozen. The only ingredients: pork and salt. Because, in L. O.'s words, when it's good barbecue, the only thing you need to put in it is your teeth.

(800) 368-2635, BishopsBBQ.com

### TIP
Find Bishop's Barbecue in the freezer section at Foodland, Food World, and Piggly Wiggly stores in Alabama as well as select Walmart locations in North Alabama.

# SNAG FRESH, FARM-RAISED SHRIMP
## MILES FROM THE COAST

In Alabama, the freshest and tastiest seafood is found mostly on the Gulf Coast, as one would expect, but if you have a hankering for fresh shrimp and don't quite have the time to drive all the way to Mobile or Orange Beach, you can find some of the best about a hundred miles north of the coast in landlocked West Alabama. Groundwater in this area has a natural salinity thanks to ancient saltwater aquifers, which makes it perfect for farming pond-raised shrimp.

Shrimp come in different varieties and sizes. West Alabama farmers almost exclusively raise Pacific white shrimp, which have a mild flavor and soak up seasonings and spices when boiled. Harvest usually starts in September and ends in October, with farmers freezing a portion of the harvest to sell throughout the year. Before heading out to one of these farms, give them a call to make sure they have shrimp available for direct-to-consumer sales.

Greene Prairie Shrimp in Boligee
(334) 507-4715, GreenePrairieAquafarm.com

Bama Pearl Shrimp in Boligee
(205) 342-0757, BamaPearlShrimp.com

Lee Jackson Farms in Hayneville
(334) 563-7563, LeeJacksonFarms.com

# PICK A PEACH
## IN CHILTON COUNTY

Halfway through a drive from Birmingham to Montgomery, a 120-foot-tall, peach-shaped water tower and numerous billboards extolling past Miss Peach Queens welcome travelers to Chilton County. It's known as the peach capital of Alabama for good reason. Its farmers produce more than two-thirds of the state's peach crop.

During peach season, which runs from May to September, Durbin Farms Market, Peach Park, and Todd's Produce & Gifts offer a wide variety of fresh Chilton County peaches, and these roadside stands are conveniently located just off the interstate. If you prefer a peaceful drive past peach farms, detour onto US Highway 31 or Alabama Highway 22, which are lined with orchards in the rural part of the county. Some of those farms have roadside stands offering baskets of perfectly ripe peaches picked earlier that day.

Peach Park, 2300 Seventh St. S., Clanton, AL 35046
(205) 755-2065, PeachParkClanton.com

Durbin Farms Market, 2130 Seventh St. S., Clanton, AL 35045
(205) 755-1672, DurbinFarms.com

Todd's Produce & Gifts, 2230 Seventh St. S., Clanton, AL 35046
(205) 294-5157, ToddsProduce.com

# TASTE-TEST GOAT CHEESE
## AT BELLE CHEVRE

Wisconsin may be famous for its cheeses made from cow's milk, but Belle Chevre in Elkmont is carving out its own niche in the dairy case with cheese made from goat's milk. Housed in a renovated cotton warehouse that was built more than one hundred years ago, Belle Chevre Creamery is the starting point for nationally and internationally acclaimed goat cheese and a slew of associated products, such as cream cheese and cheesecakes.

Taste-test the award-winning creations at the attached Cheese Shop and Tasting Room built to resemble a French cafe. While goat cheese purists will enjoy the Chevre de Provence, other offerings are more suited to Southern sensibilities, such as the Pimento Chevre or the Southern Belle, a goat cheese infused with bourbon-soaked pecans. For cheese fiends, make a meal of it! The Tasting Room serves lunch Tuesdays through Saturdays. Try the five-cheese grilled cheese or the grilled ham sandwich with fig chevre. Finish it off with chevre ice cream and the chevre cheesecake, a previous Best Dessert award-winner at the Dairy Innovation Awards in Switzerland.

18849 Upper Fort Hampton Rd., Elkmont, AL 35620
(256) 732-3577, BelleChevre.com

✓

# TRY THE FRIED GREEN TOMATOES
## AT IRONDALE CAFE

*Fried Green Tomatoes* may well be the most highly acclaimed film named after a deep-fried fruit . . . or are tomatoes a vegetable? Botany aside, the 1991 movie starring Kathy Bates and Jessica Tandy was based on the novel *Fried Green Tomatoes at the Whistle Stop Cafe* written by Birmingham native Fannie Flagg. Owned by her aunt, Bess Fortenberry, the real-life Irondale Cafe loosely served as Flagg's inspiration for the cafe featured in her novel.

Fortenberry sold the meat-and-three cafe in 1973, but its trademark fried green tomatoes have remained a mainstay. Cafe cooks fry up about eight hundred green tomato slices daily, alongside other downhome favorites, such as fried catfish, fried okra, and buttermilk fried chicken. Wash it all down with a bottled Coke or Grapico, an Alabama original grape-flavored soda.

Irondale Cafe is open for lunch every day of the week except Saturdays, so plan your trip accordingly.

1906 First Ave. N., Irondale, AL 35210
(205) 956-5258, IrondaleCafe.com

# WATCH OUT FOR THE GHOST
## AT HUGGIN' MOLLY'S

Before it was the name of a popular Abbeville restaurant, the legend of Huggin' Molly sent shivers down the spines of the town's children. As the story goes, children who stayed out too late would encounter Huggin' Molly, a seven-foot-tall ghost woman shrouded in black with a black hat. When they least expected, Molly would run up behind them, wrap them in a big hug, and let out a blood-curdling scream.

Lifelong Abbeville resident and businessman Jimmy Rane, known as Yella Fella for a character he portrayed in commercials for his YellaWood lumber company, borrowed Huggin' Molly's name for his downtown restaurant. The eatery's motto is "Frozen in the '50s," which is played out with an old-time soda fountain counter and authentic movie posters and memorabilia from the '50s, including the prop gun used in *Old Yeller.* Open daily for lunch and Thursday through Saturday for dinner, the restaurant has a simple menu. I suggest the Molly's Fingers with Comeback Sauce and a milkshake or a malt. For dinner, try Mr. Tony's Spaghetti, named for Jimmy's late father, who was a restaurateur and Italian immigrant.

129 Kirkland St., Abbeville, AL 36310
(334) 585-7000, HugginMollys.com

# PEEL A SATSUMA
## AT SESSIONS FARM MARKET

Satsumas are a variety of mandarin orange and certainly distinctive among their citrus relatives. While tart, a sweetness balances the sharp citrus flavor. Plus, the easy-to-peel skin and seedless flesh make this juicy fruit a perfect and nutritious treat for children. One bite into a satsuma and you'll be reaching for a napkin to wipe the juice dripping from your chin.

First introduced to the United States from Japan in the late 1800s, satsuma orchards proved profitable for South Alabama farmers at the turn of the nineteenth century, but bad winters and the Great Depression decimated the industry, making satsumas scarce by the 1930s. Thankfully, satsumas have made a comeback recently, and that's a benefit for everyone's taste buds.

While satsuma orchards dot the landscape in South Alabama, Sessions Farm arguably grows more than any other farm in the state. The Sessions Farm Market is sure to be fully stocked with satsumas when they're in season, which is usually from mid-October to early January.

8971 Grand Bay Wilmer Rd. S., Grand Bay, AL 36541
(251) 865-0455, Facebook.com/SessionsProduce

HANK WILLIAMS

1923   1953

# MUSIC AND ENTERTAINMENT

# EXPERIENCE THE COURTROOM DRAMA
## TO KILL A MOCKINGBIRD IN MONROEVILLE

Pulitzer Prize–winning author Harper Lee drew on her experiences of growing up in rural Monroeville to write her acclaimed 1960 novel *To Kill a Mockingbird*. The movie by the same name earned three Academy Awards in 1963, including Best Adapted Screenplay and Best Actor for Gregory Peck, who played the role of father and lawyer Atticus Finch.

While you're sure to enjoy reading the book or watching the movie, nothing is as moving as seeing the drama played out in the original Monroeville courthouse that inspired the American literary classic. Since 1991, talented amateur actors have powerfully re-created scenes from *To Kill a Mockingbird*, leaving audiences in awe. The play begins outdoors before moving inside the courtroom for Act II. During the transition, a jury of audience members is selected, and keeping with the laws of 1960, only white males over the age of eighteen are eligible.

Annual performances are held Fridays and Saturdays starting in mid-April and ending in mid-May.

31 N. Alabama Ave., Monroeville, AL 36460
(251) 743-3386, ToKillaMockingbird.com/the-play

## DID YOU KNOW?

Monroeville is considered the literary capital
of Alabama, but not just because of Pulitzer Prize
winner Harper Lee. Nine other authors, including
Truman Capote and Pulitzer Prize winner Cynthia
Tucker, called Monroeville home. Fourteen bronze
sculptures adorn the courthouse grounds to honor
the city's ten acclaimed writers.

Find out more at MonroevilleMainStreet.com/
Literary-Capital-Bronze-Sculpture-Trail.

# LISTEN TO MUSIC LEGENDS
## WITH MUSCLE SHOALS SOUND

The music of the 1960s defined a generation. While the Beatles invaded and Detroit churned out Motown hits, FAME Recording Studios and its gritty, bluesy house band, the Swampers, lured popular artists to record in Northwest Alabama.

Owned by legendary music producer Rick Hall, FAME Recording Studios became famous for its Muscle Shoals Sound. Together, Hall and the Swampers produced timeless tracks, including "Mustang Sally" by Wilson Pickett, "Do Right Woman, Do Right Man" by Aretha Franklin, "Tell Mama" by Etta James, and "Patches" by Clarence Carter. In its sixty-year history, the studio recorded or published records with a combined 350 million copies sold worldwide.

In 1969, the Swampers opened Muscle Shoals Sound Studio, their own recording studio. Their first album was Cher's *3614 Jackson Highway*, named for the new studio's address. Other artists who recorded there include the Rolling Stones, Linda Ronstadt, Rod Stewart, James Brown, Willie Nelson, Boz Scaggs, and Art Garfunkel. Both studios offer tours. Plus, true music lovers will also enjoy touring the nearby Alabama Music Hall of Fame and the birthplace of W.C. Handy, the "Father of the Blues."

**FAME Recording Studios**
603 E. Avalon Ave., Muscle Shoals, AL 35661
(256) 381-0801, ext. 1
famestudios.com

**Muscle Shoals Sound Studio**
3614 Jackson Hwy., Sheffield, AL 35660
(256) 978-5151, MuscleShoalsSoundStudio.org

**Alabama Music Hall of Fame**
617 Hwy. 72 W., Tuscumbia, AL 35674
(256) 381-4417, alamhof.org

**W.C. Handy Birthplace, Museum & Library**
620 W. College St., Florence, AL
(256) 760-6434, visitflorenceal.com/things_to_do/w-c-handy-
birthplace-museum-library

# SING ALONG
## WITH THE MIGHTY WURLITZER

Catching a flick at the historic Alabama Theatre in downtown Birmingham is a movie-going experience unlike any other in the state. If the stately staircases, statues, and carvings in the lobby don't set it apart enough, you'll notice the difference inside the cinema when a portion of the stage floor gives way, and a behemoth pipe organ ascends from the theater's underbelly. Lovingly referred to as "Big Bertha" or "The Mighty Wurlitzer," the organ hearkens back to a bygone era when a live organist played scores to accompany silent movies.

The theater opened in 1927 with its custom-built Wurlitzer. The Alabama chapter of the American Theatre Organ Society bought the dilapidated property in the 1980s to save "Big Bertha." Thanks to the group's restoration efforts, the organ once again delights audiences in the pristinely restored theater. The organist often plays to sell-out crowds of two thousand people during the theater's popular sing-along showings of such classic movies as *Casablanca* and seasonal favorites, especially at Christmastime.

1817 Third Ave. N., Birmingham, AL 35203
(205) 252-2262, AlabamaTheatre.com

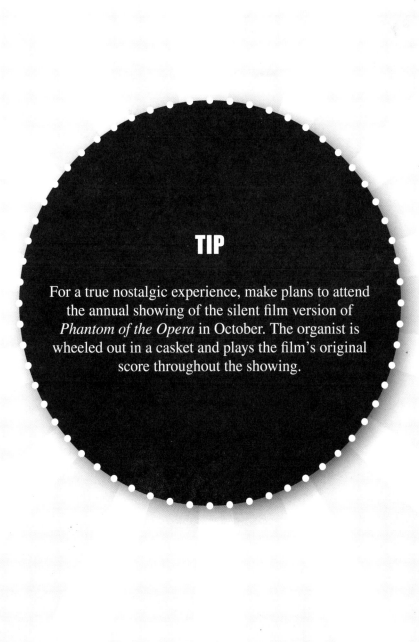

# TIP

For a true nostalgic experience, make plans to attend the annual showing of the silent film version of *Phantom of the Opera* in October. The organist is wheeled out in a casket and plays the film's original score throughout the showing.

# SPEND A DAY
## AT AN ART MUSEUM

Trappist monk Thomas Merton once said, "Art enables us to find ourselves and lose ourselves at the same time." In the numerous art museums across Alabama, you'll find plenty of ways to lose yourself among the array of simple, complex, sophisticated, unrefined, harmonious, and dissonant art collections.

The Birmingham Museum of Art seeps with true metropolitan flair. Located on nearly four acres in the city's historic district, it boasts a collection of more than twenty-seven thousand pieces ranging from ancient times to the modern era. The Mobile Museum of Art displays the works of regional, national, and international artists among its ten thousand pieces and is the only accredited art museum in South Alabama. Along with gorgeous artwork, enjoy the beautiful parks surrounding the Montgomery Museum of Fine Arts and the Huntsville Museum of Art. The ancient Martin Petroglyph, with Native American carvings from a thousand years ago, is preserved at the Tennessee Valley Museum of Art, and the Wiregrass Museum of Art is located in Dothan's historic water and electric building downtown.

**Birmingham Museum of Art**
2000 Rev. Abraham Woods Jr. Blvd.
Birmingham, AL 35203
(205) 254-2565, ArtsBMA.org

**Mobile Museum of Art**
4850 Museum Dr., Mobile, AL 36608
(251) 208-5200, MobileMuseumOfArt.com

**Montgomery Museum of Fine Arts**
1 Museum Dr., Montgomery, AL 36117
(334) 625-4333, MMFA.org

**Huntsville Museum of Art**
300 Church St. S., Huntsville, AL 35801
(256) 535-4350, HSVMuseum.org

**Tennessee Valley Museum of Art**
511 N. Water St., Tuscumbia, AL 35674
(256) 383-0533, TVAA.net

**Wiregrass Museum of Art**
126 Museum Ave., Dothan, AL 36303
(334) 794-3871, WiregrassMuseum.org

# BLOW A GLASS ORNAMENT
## AT ORBIX HOT GLASS

Cal and Christy Breed have perfected the ancient art of glassblowing, and they share their talents at their Orbix Hot Glass studio just outside Fort Payne. The studio is located on twenty-six acres of land that borders the Little River Canyon National Preserve, and the Breeds gain inspiration from the natural beauty that surrounds them to create exquisitely delicate glass pieces. Some are meant to be looked at, such as wall hangings and ornaments, while others are fully functional, for example, pitchers, vases, and decanters. Yet all are pieces of art.

The Breeds love sharing their passion for glassblowing. Their company has grown to include a team of glassblowers who handcraft each piece, and they teach aspiring glassblowers during classes at their studio. Guests may try their hands at creating a glass ornament, flower, or tumbler. The classes can be a bit humbling, but it does help that customers come away with a new appreciation for the expertise and skill glassblowing requires.

3869 County Rd. 275, Fort Payne, AL 35967
(256) 523-3188, OrbixHotGlass.com

# COUNT THE TREE CARVINGS
## IN ORR PARK

Orr Park in Montevallo covers forty acres along Shoal Creek. While the park is beautiful in its own right, the work of one imaginative man sets it apart from other similar civic developments.

In the 1990s, coal miner Tim Tingle noticed that storm-damaged cedar trees along the park's walking trail were dying, and he decided to give them new life as canvases for his carvings. Now a fanciful forest of funny faces and comical creatures, the tree-filled trail is affectionately known as Tinglewood. It's a delight to traipse through Tinglewood and count the carvings, from a snake-eating unicorn and gnomes to dragons and the Tree King.

While he may not have intended to, Tingle's creations have inspired other wood carvers. Because of his work, Orr Park hosts an annual one-day Tinglewood Festival in the fall to celebrate all kinds of woodworking crafts.

277 Park Dr., Montevallo, AL 35115
(205) 665-2555, CityOfMontevallo.com/288/Orr-Park

# ATTEND
## AN ALABAMA FESTIVAL

Alabama festivals celebrate everything from music, legumes, sausage, and Scottish heritage to poisonous plants and venomous animals. Attending just one of these festivals can finish off your bucket list, but for you die-hards in the crowd, take this as an opportunity to experience more than just one hundred things in the great state of Alabama.

## National Peanut Festival
Held annually in Dothan to celebrate the peanut harvest.
NationalPeanutFestival.com

## Southeast Alabama Highland Games
Celebrate Scottish heritage by throwing phone poles,
or cabers, end-over-end along with other feats of strength.
Also in Dothan in March.
WiregrassHighlandGames.com

## Opp Rattlesnake Rodeo
Snake shows, snake races, and snake safety presentations.
Hosted in the city of Opp every March.
OppRattlesnakeRodeo.com

## Tennessee Valley Old Time Fiddlers Convention
Three days of pickin' and grinnin' capped off with crowning the
Alabama State Fiddle Champion. Held every October in Athens.
tvotfc.org

## World's Largest Peanut Boil
Eating boiled peanuts must be on your Alabama bucket list. The
city of Luverne boils tons of them during this event every fall.
Search for it on Facebook.

## Conecuh Sausage Festival
Sure, the name makes you snicker, but the folks in
Conecuh County are serious about their sausage. See why
on the third Saturday of October.
facebook.com/EvergreenSausageFestival

## Poke Salat Festival
Raw poke salat, a type of weed, is poisonous, but after
boiling it a couple of times, it makes for a tasty side dish,
unique to the South and Appalachian regions. Try some during
this annual event in May in Arab.
DowntownArab.com/PokeSalat.html

# JUMP ON BOARD THE TRAIN
## AT THE HEART OF DIXIE RAILROAD MUSEUM

The Heart of Dixie Railroad Museum serves as a tribute to a bygone era when the sounds of train whistles and chugging railcars were heard in nearly every community. Partially housed in a restored train depot, the museum boasts a collection of railroad artifacts and memorabilia as well as standard and narrow gauge locomotives, railcars, and cabooses.

While the museum is enjoyable for train enthusiasts and laymen alike, the real treat of the Heart of Dixie Railroad Museum is hopping on and punching your ticket for a ride down memory lane. Every Saturday a restored vintage train takes riders on a run down a portion of the former L&N Alabama Mineral Railroad, originally built in 1891. As the Calera & Shelby Railroad winds through the calming terrain of Shelby County's scenic forests, the ride is a nice reminder of simpler times before interstates ushered in an age of road rage. Themed events, such as Wild West Day or North Pole Express during Christmastime, make the train rides even more memorable.

1919 Ninth St., Calera, AL 35040
(205) 757-8383, hodrrm.org

# SEE THE SHRIMP BOATS
## DURING THE BLESSING OF THE FLEET IN BAYOU LA BATRE

If the scenery of Bayou La Batre reminds you of Forrest Gump leaping off his shrimp boat to joyously welcome Lieutenant Dan, there's good reason. Portions of the 1994 movie were filmed in this little fishing village south of Mobile. Connected to the Gulf of Mexico by the bayou, fishing and shipbuilding are important industries in the town known as the "Seafood Capital of Alabama."

Founded in 1786 by a Frenchman, the Catholic faith has influenced the town's culture, which is especially evident in May during the annual Blessing of the Fleet. Saint Margaret Catholic Church, built along the bayou, serves as the hub of the two-day event, which features a smorgasbord of seafood cooked by locals and Asian cuisine prepared by the city's Vietnamese, Laotian, and Cambodian immigrants. To culminate the celebration, the archbishop of Mobile boards the lead boat of a parade down the bayou, sprinkling holy water along the route and offering prayers for all those involved in the seafood industry.

13790 S. Wintzell Ave., Bayou La Batre, AL 36509
(251) 824-2415, FleetBlessing.org

# PICK THE PERFECT PUMPKIN

In Alabama, the sweltering heat of summer often lasts through September, which makes that first October hint of chill in the air all the more welcome. When forecasted highs finally top out in the high seventies, it's time to welcome fall by picking the perfect pumpkin from a local farm.

Pumpkins are a tough crop to grow in Alabama's weather, but there are plenty of patches where farmers have perfected the art of growing gourds. These farms offer much more than just pumpkins. With corn mazes, corn cribs, hay bale art, hay rides, jumping pillows, tube slides, petting zoos, country cafes, and other attractions, there's enough to keep you busy from sunrise to sunset.

### Tate Farms Cotton Pickin' Pumpkins
Pose for a picture in the pumpkin house.
8414 Moores Mill Rd., Meridianville, AL 35759
(256) 828-8288, TateFarmsAL.com

### 4D Farm
Get lost in the massive corn maze.
7182 County Rd. 703, Cullman, AL 35055
(256) 775-2924, 4DFamilyFarm.com

### Aplin Farms
Pick a couple of sunflowers for a farm-fresh fall bouquet.
2729 N. County Rd. 49, Dothan, AL 36305
(334) 726-5104, facebook.com/AplinFarms

### Dream Field Farms
Stay for the night in one of the newly built cabins
overlooking the lake.
6376 US Hwy. 82, Fitzpatrick, AL 36029
(334) 534-6976, DreamFieldFarms.com

### Backyard Orchards
Sample each flavor of their homemade fudge.
6585 Hwy. 431 N., Eufaula, AL 36027
(334) 695-5875, BackyardOrchards.com

# STOP BY
## 1818 FARMS AND THE TOWN OF MOORESVILLE

The city of Mooresville is just two miles off Interstate 65 on the way to Huntsville, but most folks don't even know it's there. A quaint, charming little town with narrow streets and colonial-inspired homes, Mooresville was founded in 1818. The town's sixty residents maintain the square and its antebellum stagecoach inn and tavern, brick church, and post office. Houses do not have mailboxes; residents just walk to the post office during business hours to pick up their mail.

While Mooresville is a secret gem, it's drawn more visitors recently thanks to the McCrary family, who are sixth-generation Mooresvillians. In 2011, they opened 1818 Farms on the edge of town, an agritourism attraction specializing in floriculture. Folks come from neighboring cities and even across state lines to attend the farm's events, including farm-to-fork dinners, bouquet-making workshops, and exercise classes. The McCrarys also host photography courses, and with hens, pigs, goats, and babydoll sheep being raised alongside the flowers at 1818 Farms, there are plenty of snapshot-worthy moments to capture.

1818 Farms, 24889 Lauderdale St., Mooresville, AL 35649
(256) 489-0777, 1818Farms.com

# THROW SHOES OVER THE LINE
## AT SPECTRE

Shooting a movie in Alabama usually requires building sets, which crews ultimately dismantle before leaving town, but when a crew created the fictional town of Spectre for Tim Burton's film *Big Fish*, they left the set standing at the request of the landowners. In the movie, the town of Spectre was an idyllic place, with lush lawns where no one wore shoes. When visitors stumbled upon the settlement, Spectre's citizens would force them to stay by taking their shoes, tying the laces together, and throwing them over a high rope.

Today, a street of the fictional town of Spectre remains on the very real Jackson Lake Island, a sliver of land surrounded by the Alabama River. While the buildings have taken on a ghostly feel, that high rope still exists, and it's always covered with shoes left by tourists. If you prefer to keep your shoes on your feet, simply enjoy taking photos as goats graze around the old church at the end of the street. Or bring a fishing pole. Jackson Lake Island is a great place to fish from the riverbanks.

Cypress Ln., Millbrook, AL 36054
(334) 430-7963, facebook.com/JacksonLakeIsland

# RIDE
## A RIVERBOAT

Fourteen major rivers flow through Alabama. These waterways are so important that they're featured on the state's official seal. Before blacktop connected states, rivers and rails were the main forms of interstate commerce. Riverboats were a common sight, carrying passengers as well as raw materials and manufactured goods from one river town to another.

Thankfully, a few of these queens of the water still operate in Alabama, although their purpose now is purely entertainment. In Montgomery, the *Harriott II* ushers riders down and back up the Alabama River with fantastic sunset views during dinner or jazz cruises. The *Bama Belle* makes its home at Medeiros Point on the Black Warrior River in Tuscaloosa. Choose the Lock-Thru Cruise to experience a ride through the Oliver Lock and Dam. And the *Perdido Queen* paddles its way through the Mobile River with stunning city views of Mobile. For those who prefer a tour rather than a ride, there's also the *Snagboat Montgomery*, a steam-powered sternwheeler docked in Pickensville in West Alabama.

***Harriott II* Riverboat Ticket Office**
255 Commerce St., Montgomery, AL 36104
(334) 625-2100, FunInMontgomery.com/parks-items/harriott-ii-
riverboat

***Bama Belle* Paddleboat Riverboat**
1 Greensboro Ave., Tuscaloosa, AL 35401
(205) 275-0560, BamaBelle.org

***Perdido Queen***
1 S. Water St., Mobile, AL 36602
(251) 948-6611, PerdidoQueen.com

**Tom Bevill Visitor Center with *Snagboat Montgomery***
1382 Lock and Dam Rd., Pickensville, AL 35447
(205) 373-8705

# CELEBRATE THE MUSIC
## OF HANK WILLIAMS

Legendary country music artist Hank Williams honed his musical skills growing up in Butler and Montgomery counties. He learned gospel hymns from his mother, an organist for a Baptist church, and blues tunes from African American street musician Rufus "Tee Tot" Payne. During his 1949 performance at the Grand Ole Opry in Nashville, the audience insisted on six encores. Such hits as "Your Cheatin' Heart," "Hey Good Lookin'," and "I'm So Lonesome I Could Cry" helped him rack up more than thirty-five Top 10 singles.

Williams's life was tragically cut short. At age twenty-nine, he died of a heart attack brought on by addiction problems. More than twenty thousand people attended his funeral at the Municipal Auditorium inside Montgomery's City Hall. His memory is kept alive with numerous tributes. Every year thousands of visitors stop by Williams's final resting place at Oakwood Annex Cemetery in Montgomery. A statue of Williams welcomes pedestrians to Montgomery's Riverfront Park, and the Hank Williams Museum downtown is a short, one-block walk from the statue. His boyhood home in Georgiana is now a museum, which hosts the annual Hank Williams Festival.

**Hank Williams Grave at Oakwood Annex Cemetery**
1304 Upper Wetumpka Rd., Montgomery, AL 36107

**Hank Williams Statue at Riverfront Park**
355 Commerce St., Montgomery, AL 36104

**Hank Williams Museum**
118 Commerce St., Montgomery, AL 36104
(334) 262-3600, TheHankWilliamsMuseum.net

**Hank Williams Boyhood Home and Museum**
127 Rose St., Georgiana, AL 36033
(334) 376-2555, HankMuseum.com, HankWilliamsFestival.com

# GET UNDERGROUND
## AT CATHEDRAL CAVERNS

The great cathedrals of the world stand hundreds of feet tall, soaring toward the heavens with impressive vaulted ceilings supported by massive, decorative columns. Cathedral Caverns in Northeast Alabama earned its name for its naturally occurring characteristics that mimic these religious spaces. The ceiling of the cave's largest room towers 123 feet above spelunkers, making it large enough to fit an eleven-story building. The impressive rock formations of the stalagmite forest resemble church columns, including the stalagmite known as Goliath. With a circumference of 245 feet and a height of 45 feet, it's one of the largest stalagmites in the world.

Private landowner Jacob Gurley opened Cathedral Caverns to the public in the 1950s, but it didn't become an official state park until 2000. The park is now run by the Alabama Department of Conservation and Natural Resources, and tourists can experience the cave's breathtaking underground scenery of waterfalls, rivers, and limestone geology with a ninety-minute tour that covers 1.5 miles.

637 Cave Rd., Woodville, AL 35769
(256) 728-8193, alapark.com/cathedral-caverns-state-park

# MARVEL AT THE ARRAY OF ART
## AT LOWE MILL

Cotton was once king in Alabama. As the textile industry waned, numerous mills and factories were left empty across the state. Famed genetics researcher and Huntsville resident Jim Hudson, whose companies helped map the human genome, bought one of these empty cotton mills in 2001 and transformed it into the largest privately owned arts community in the United States.

Husdon's Lowe Mill ARTS and Entertainment encompasses more than one hundred thousand square feet with 148 working studios. The space also houses six galleries, a theater, performance venues, restaurants, a coffee shop, and a whiskey distillery, and the galleries feature more than just painters. Weavers, potters, sculptors, instrument-makers, photographers, and quilters are among the more than four hundred displaying artists. In addition to using studio space, Lowe Mill's participating makers teach classes and workshops to inspire others, and they sell their wares during public hours Wednesday through Saturday.

2211 Seminole Dr., Huntsville, AL 35805
(256) 533-0399, LoweMill.net

# CATCH A MOONPIE
## DURING MARDI GRAS

For most Americans, Mardi Gras is synonymous with New Orleans. While the Big Easy hosts the nation's largest Fat Tuesday celebration, Mobile lays claim to hosting the nation's first Mardi Gras way back in 1703 when the city was the capital of Louisiana.

More than three hundred years later, Mardi Gras celebrations have expanded into a month's worth of parties in seemingly every city, town, and settlement in both Mobile County and neighboring Baldwin County. Staying true to their French roots, mystic societies in Alabama's coastal towns are charged with coordinating parades, balls, and other Mardi Gras events.

While you have to know somebody who knows somebody to receive a coveted ball invitation, parades are open to the public. You'll be pelted by more projectile MoonPies and beads than your hands can hold, so remember to bring a bag or two to gather all your parade loot.

MobileMask.com/parade-schedule.html

*Photo courtesy Caleb Hicks*

# SPORTS AND RECREATION

# CHEER ON THE BISCUITS
## AND TAKE HOME A HAT

Minor league baseball boasts the most creative team names, and Alabama's capital city has one of the best—the Montgomery Biscuits. The merchandise and atmosphere at Riverwalk Stadium set this team apart from the others. Half the stadium is a renovated train station built in 1898. Left field is bordered by the railroad track, and it never fails to elicit cheers from fans when a homerun ball nicks a passing train car. How many ballparks can offer their mascot as a menu item at concessions? Just remember to order your biscuit with a piece of fried chicken smothered in Alaga syrup, a local favorite bottled just down the street at Whitfield Foods.

The stadium's Biscuit Basket store offers the best souvenirs, featuring "Monty," a smiling buttermilk biscuit with a pat of butter for a tongue. I'm partial to the Monty cap in the team's official colors of butter and blue.

200 Coosa St., Montgomery, AL 36104
(334) 819-7483, milb.com/Montgomery

# HEAR THE ROAR
# OF ENGINES
## AT TALLADEGA

Talladega Superspeedway is the track of dreams for NASCAR. Every spring and fall the fields surrounding the track overflow with RVs and campers as more than 150,000 fans flood the speedway for a heart-pounding, eardrum-numbing weekend of racing at the longest and often fastest track in the country.

Those fans are hungry to be a part of the track's storied history. It's where Jimmie Johnson earned his 2011 victory by driving .002 seconds faster than second place, where Dale Earnhardt racked up his record ten career victories, and where Ron Bouchard won by a foot over Darrell Waltrip in 1981. It's the place where brothers Donnie and Bobby Allison became racing legends and where fathers and sons Dale and Dale Jr. and Bill and Chase Elliott were inscribed into the history books as champions. With drivers reaching speeds over 190 miles an hour, driving three cars wide in thirty-three-degree curves, there's sure to be many more thrilling moments captured between "Gentlemen, start your engines!" and the checkered flag.

3366 Speedway Blvd., Talladega, AL 35160
(256) 761-4976, TalladegaSuperspeedway.com

# HONE YOUR NATURE PHOTOGRAPHY SKILLS
## AT LITTLE RIVER CANYON

The eighteen-mile Little River Canyon offers spectacular views of the Appalachian Plateau every season of the year, and best of all hiking boots are not required! Eight overlooks along an eleven-mile scenic drive on Alabama Highway 176 in DeKalb and Cherokee counties make it the perfect place to capture breathtaking panoramas of the canyon landscape carved by Little River, which runs atop Lookout Mountain. If you stop by the Little River Canyon Center, a boardwalk provides an easy trek to see Little River Falls.

The preserve's backcountry area includes twenty-three miles of dirt roads for horseback riding, and the river is a popular spot for adventurous kayakers. For those who prefer to lace up their hiking boots, plenty of trails are available to explore. Along the way, keep your eyes peeled for the green pitcher plant, a rare carnivorous plant that eats insects. If you find one, feel free to name your discovery something exotic, for example, Audrey III, and snap lots of pictures, but remember to leave the plant be.

4322 Little River Trail NE, Fort Payne, AL 35967
(256) 845-9605, ext. 20, nps.gov/liri

## TIP

You can view numerous waterfalls from the scenic overlooks, but these can dry up during an arid summer, so plan your trip accordingly.

# PICK A SIDE:
## WAR EAGLE OR ROLL TIDE

Alabamians ask two questions when they meet someone new: Where do you go to church, and who do you root for? They don't elaborate on the second question. It should be obvious they're asking whether you're a fan of the University of Alabama or Auburn University. Down here, college football reigns supreme, and the rivalry between the Tigers and the Crimson Tide is fierce. You have to pick a side—War Eagle or Roll Tide.

Bryant-Denny Stadium in Tuscaloosa impresses with its Walk of Champions displaying Alabama's numerous SEC and national championships. Auburn's Jordan-Hare Stadium becomes the state's fifth-largest city on game days, and the traditional pregame flight of the eagle is sure to get you on your feet.

Catch a game at both stadiums. To really feel the strength of the rivalry, watch the teams head-to-head during the Iron Bowl, traditionally played the Saturday after Thanksgiving.

Bryant-Denny Stadium, 920 Bryant Dr., Tuscaloosa, AL 35401
(205) 348-2262, RollTide.com

Jordan-Hare Stadium, 251 S. Donahue Dr., Auburn, AL 36849
(855) 282-2010 (option 3), AuburnTigers.com

# PLAY OR RELAX
## AT PURSELL FARMS

Located an hour outside of Birmingham, Pursell Farms is a welcome reprieve from big-city living. This one-of-a-kind luxurious resort drips with touches of Southern hospitality thanks to David and Ellen Pursell, the fourth generation of the family to make a living off the land.

Under David's guidance, the family business has transformed into a must-visit destination. In 2003 he oversaw the creation of FarmLinks, the world's only research and demonstration golf course, but a round of golf is just the beginning of what you can experience on Pursell Farm's 3,200 acres. Orvis Shooting Grounds offers lessons in shooting clays and fly casting. There's a swimming pool, bike rentals, horseback riding, trips to Lay Lake, and exercise classes. If you seek relaxation, you'll find it at the on-site spa or with a meal at one of three restaurants. Accommodation options are numerous, from the newly built inn and cottages to renovated, historic antebellum homes.

386 Talladega Springs Rd., Sylacauga, AL 35151
(256) 208-7600, PursellFarms.com

# PLAY A ROUND OR TWO
## ON THE ROBERT TRENT
## JONES GOLF TRAIL

No matter your handicap, the Robert Trent Jones Golf Trail provides challenging, professional-level golf with beautiful, breathtaking backdrops. Soak in the serenity of the most iconic spot on the trail with a round on the Judge course at the Capitol Hill site in Prattville. The tee on the first hole sits atop a plateau, as the fairway slopes drastically downward to a dramatic view of Gun Island Chute, part of the Alabama River. The stunning scenery is sure to ease the pain of chalking up a double bogey on the tough par-four hole.

After a round of eighteen, try one of the other courses at Capitol Hill. The Senator is a links-style course that has hosted numerous professional tournaments, and the Legislator is a traditional course with numerous pine trees playing defense against getting your ball in the hole. Or load up the clubs and travel to one of the other ten RTJ sites that dot the state. In all, there are 468 championship holes on twenty-six courses.

*rtjgolf.com*

| | |
|---|---|
| **Capitol Hill** | **Magnolia Grove** |
| 2600 Constitution Ave. | 7001 Magnolia Grove Pkwy. |
| Prattville, AL 36066 | Mobile, AL 36618 |
| (334) 285-1114 | (251) 645-0075 |
| | |
| **Cambrian Ridge** | **Oxmoor Valley** |
| 101 SunBelt Pkwy. | 100 Sunbelt Pkwy. |
| Greenville, AL 36037 | Birmingham, AL 35211 |
| (334) 382-9787 | (205) 942-1177 |
| | |
| **Grand National** | **Ross Bridge** |
| 3000 Robert Trent Jones Tr. | 4000 Grand Ave. |
| Opelika, AL 36801 | Hoover, AL 35226 |
| (334) 749-9042 | (205) 949-3085 |
| | |
| **Hampton Cove** | **Silver Lakes** |
| 450 Old Hwy. 431 | 1 Sunbelt Pkwy. |
| Owens Crossroads, AL 35763 | Glencoe, AL 35905 |
| (256) 551-1818 | (256) 892-3268 |
| | |
| **Highland Oaks** | **The Shoals** |
| 904 Royal Pkwy. | 990 Sunbelt Pkwy. |
| Dothan, AL 36305 | Muscle Shoals, AL 35661 |
| (334) 712-2820 | (256) 446-5111 |
| | |
| **Lakewood Golf Club** | |
| One Grand Blvd. | |
| Point Clear, AL 36564 | |
| (251) 990-6312 | |

# SEARCH FOR GLOWING CREATURES
## AT DISMALS CANYON

A dizzying array of flora and fauna can be found in the waterfalls, sandstone gorge, cave formations, and forested lands of Dismals Canyon. One of the oldest primeval forests east of the Mississippi River, the canyon has received national recognition for its biological and geological diversity. On the 1.5-mile trek through the canyon floor, hikers can see thirty of the nation's official state trees, along with 350 species of exotic flora.

To see one of the true wonders of Dismals Canyon, though, you have to wait until dark. Once the sun goes to sleep, the canyon walls come to life with glowing larvae, which locals call Dismalites. On a clear night, the glowing worms make it impossible to differentiate between the night sky and the canyon walls. These are the only bioluminescent insects native to North America, and across the globe their only habitats aside from this canyon are in Australia and New Zealand.

901 Hwy. 8, Phil Campbell, AL 35581
(205) 993-4559, DismalsCanyon.com

# TAKE IN A RACE
## AT BARBER MOTORSPORTS

Stepping onto the grounds at Barber Motorsports feels like entering a beautifully manicured park, complete with impressive sculptures, pine forests, and water features covering 880 acres. It seems almost accidental that the space includes a museum and a 2.38-mile road course, where IndyCars and motorcycles race at speeds averaging more than 115 miles an hour. That's the way Alabama native George W. Barber wanted it when he started construction on his racetrack that's been called the "Augusta National of Motorsports."

The museum houses the world's largest collection of motorcycles, with more than nine hundred displayed, the earliest dating back to 1904. It's the perfect place to start your trip to Barber Motorsports on a race weekend. Whether it's the IndyCar Series's Grand Prix, a MotoAmerica motorcycle race, or a contest of vintage race cars, spectators spread out across the grassy banks of the track with picnic blankets and lawn chairs to enjoy the fast-paced sport. Turns eight and eleven offer the most complete view of the track's seventeen turns, but fans can also enjoy the race from turns two, three, or fourteen.

6040 Barber Motorsports Pkwy., Birmingham, AL 35094
(205) 298-9040, BarberRacingEvents.com

# TAKE IN THE VIEW
## ATOP MOUNT CHEAHA

Jutting out from the prolific pine trees of the Talladega National Forest, Mount Cheaha towers over the rest of Alabama. Reaching 2,407 feet above sea level, the mountain is the state's highest point, offering an awesome vista of the Appalachian foothills.

The observation deck of Bunker Tower is one of the best places to take in the view. The Civilian Conservation Corps built the tower on the very tip-top of the mountain in Cheaha State Park, and it now serves as a museum to the workers of President FDR's New Deal program. The scenery is also stunning from the park's Bald Rock overlook, which is an easy hike for people of all ages thanks to a quarter-mile, wheelchair-accessible wooden walkway.

If you prefer a challenge, the park offers numerous trails of varying degrees of difficulty for hiking, backpacking, and even mountain biking. A section of the hundred-mile Pinhoti Trail meanders through the park's dense forests, and mountain bikers descend on the Cheaha Express Trail annually for the Cheaha Challenge mountain bike race.

19644 Hwy. 281, Delta, AL 36258
(256) 488-5115, alapark.com/cheaha-state-park

# TEST YOUR LONG JUMP SKILLS
## AT JESSE OWENS MEMORIAL PARK

At the 1936 Olympics in Berlin, track-and-field star Jesse Owens became the first American to win four gold medals, besting the field in the one hundred meters, two hundred meters, long jump, and four by one hundred meter relay. No one would match Owens's record of four track-and-field gold medals for forty-eight years, and he achieved these feats as an African American under the unwelcoming eye of Germany's chancellor, Adolf Hitler.

A tribute to Owens's ground-breaking, record-setting athleticism and his community-minded spirit, the Jesse Owens Memorial Park was dedicated in 1996 in his hometown, the unincorporated community of Oakville. The day of the dedication, Owens's widow, Ruth, lit an eternal flame, built as a replica of the 1936 Olympics torch, using the torch for the 1996 Summer Olympic Games as it traveled through the state to Atlanta, Georgia.

There's much to see at the thirty-acre park, which includes a museum, a replica of the Owens home, and a statue of Owens, but be sure to stop by the long jump pit to test your skills against Owens's gold-medal distance of 26 feet, 5 5/16 inches.

7019 County Rd. 203, Danville, AL 35619
(256) 974-3636, JesseOwensMemorialPark.com

# VISIT
## NOCCALULA FALLS PARK

Noccalula Falls provides gorgeous scenery with a tragic backstory of *Romeo and Juliet* proportions. According to legend, an Indian chief and his beautiful daughter, Noccalula, lived near the falls. The young woman loved a warrior from her tribe, but her father arranged for her to marry a powerful chief of a neighboring tribe. On her wedding day, clothed in her wedding robes, Noccalula walked to the precipice of the falls and jumped to her death. Since that day, the falls have borne her name. To honor her memory, a nine-foot-tall bronze statue representing Noccalula was added to the park in 1969.

While it's a sad tale, the park offers many attractions for a pleasant visit. First is the ninety-foot-tall falls itself. A short hike off the park's Black Creek Trail onto the Gorge Trail will take you under the falls. Or stay dry by viewing the falls from the walking bridge over the creek. There's also a petting zoo, a miniature train that patrons can ride through the park, and a pioneer village.

1500 Noccalula Rd., Gadsden, AL 35904
(256) 549-4663, NoccalulaFallsPark.com

### TIP
Plan your visit during winter or spring. The area usually receives more rain during these seasons, making the waterfall that much more impressive.

# BUILD A SANDCASTLE
## ON THE BEACHES OF BALDWIN COUNTY

Alabama has only sixty miles of coastline on the Gulf of Mexico, but that's a good thing; it keeps Alabamians humble because those sixty miles are some of the most perfect beaches you'll find in the continental U.S. The beaches of Dauphin Island, Fort Morgan, Orange Beach, and Gulf Shores are covered in soft, sugar-white sand, and on calmer days the Gulf glistens with shades of emerald, amethyst, and cobalt. There's really nothing more relaxing than breathing the salt air as you dig your feet into the sand to the tune of gentle waves lapping against the shore.

The beaches are Alabama's top tourism attraction, so there are plenty of options for lodging, eating, and adventuring to fit any budget. The state-owned Gulf State Park spans three miles between Orange Beach and Gulf Shores and offers numerous accommodations, including the Lodge. Forced to close after Hurricane Ivan in 2004, the Lodge underwent a complete renovation and reopened in 2018, allowing visitors to experience the natural beauty of the state park and beaches with first-class resort amenities.

21196 E. Beach Blvd., Gulf Shores, AL 36542
(251) 540-4000, LodgeatGulfStatePark.com

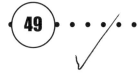

# WATCH FOR EAGLES
## AT LAKE GUNTERSVILLE STATE PARK

Surrounded by the Appalachian Mountains, Lake Guntersville offers fantastic views of water and land. The Tennessee Valley Authority created the shallow lake in 1939 along with the construction of Guntersville Dam. While it's well-known as a superior fishing lake, it's also the best place in the state to bird-watch for the US national emblem—the bald eagle.

Until recently, bald eagles had not nested in Alabama since 1949. Thanks to conservation efforts, bird-watchers now report seeing 100 to 150 of the once endangered birds in the state annually, with most of those reports coming from Lake Guntersville State Park. The Town Creek pier is the best place to catch a glimpse of the majestic raptors, but there are other sites where visitors might see them, including Minky Creek Boat Ramp, the park campground, Short Creek, and Mabrey Overlook. All are accessible by foot, but remember to bring a pair of binoculars.

1155 Lodge Dr., Guntersville, AL 35976
(256) 571-5440, AlaPark.com/lake-guntersville-state-park

## TIP

Schedule your visit for January or February to experience the park's Eagle Awareness Weekends, which include indoor seminars with birds of prey. If you plan your trip for summer, you're unlikely to see eagles, but you can enjoy watching thousands of gray bats emerge from Hambrick Cave on the Tennessee River, just a mile from Guntersville Dam.

# GAZE
## AT THE WHITE CLIFFS OF EPES AND WHITE BLUFF

Located in Alabama's Black Belt, an area named for its rich, fertile, black soils, the White Cliffs of Epes stand in stark contrast to the surrounding landscape. You can't help but notice the startling sight as you drive across the river bridge on US Highway 11 just outside the tiny town of Epes. The bridge also happens to be the best place to snap a picture of these sheer, thirty-foot-tall cliffs that stretch for about a mile along the banks of the muddy Tombigbee River. Just be mindful of other travelers when you stop your car.

The cliffs are part of the Selma Group, a series of chalk formations that are believed to have been deposited about seventy million years ago, around the same time the White Cliffs of Dover in England were created. A mere thirty-minute drive away, you can view another Selma Group outcropping in Demopolis. The town's White Bluff is best seen from the back side of the Demopolis Civic Center, and it's the backdrop for the popular Christmas on the River festival.

White Cliffs of Epes
GPS coordinates: N 32.694222, W 88.114917

Demopolis Civic Center
501 N. Commissioners Ave., Demopolis, AL 36732

# SMELL THE ROSES AND OTHER FLOWERS
## AT BELLINGRATH GARDENS

While humid and hot during the summer, one of the wonderful traits of South Alabama's climate is that it's temperate enough for flowers, trees, and shrubs to bloom year-round. And no other Alabama garden rivals the pristine beauty of the sixty-five acres at Bellingrath Gardens.

The season starts in January, when more than four hundred varieties of camellias, Alabama's official state flower, begin to bloom. In spring, the grounds are covered with flowering azaleas, followed by roses and hydrangeas in the summer. The cascading mums show during autumn is a real treat, as the flowing chrysanthemums create blankets of burnt orange, sparkling yellow, fire brick red, and creamy white. Because it rarely snows in South Alabama, Bellingrath Gardens gets into the holiday spirit every winter with its Magic Christmas in Lights. More than 1,100 decorative pieces lit with more than three million Christmas lights dot the garden's grounds for a delightful December display.

12401 Bellingrath Gardens Rd., Theodore, AL 36582
(251) 973-2217, Bellingrath.org

# MOSEY
## THROUGH A BOTANICAL GARDEN

Three of Alabama's largest cities have their own botanical gardens. Besides blankets of beautiful seasonal blooms, each boasts distinctive attractions, making them worthy walks in the park. The hundred-acre Mobile Botanical Gardens includes walking trails through a thirty-five-acre preserve of longleaf pines, Alabama's official state tree. Once covering millions of acres of the Southeast, longleaf pine forests are considered an endangered ecosystem. The Huntsville Botanical Garden features a Children's Garden with Butterfly House. Thousands of visitors attend the garden's fall Scarecrow Trail and winter Galaxy of Lights.

The crowning jewel of these gardens is found in Birmingham. Every year the Birmingham Botanical Gardens welcomes more than 350,000 people to walk the grounds free of charge, although you can also take a guided tour for a small fee. Inside, you'll find trails winding through more than twenty-five interpretive and thematic gardens, including the acclaimed Japanese Gardens, the Kaul Wildflower Garden, the Fern Glade, and the Southern Living Garden, designed by the popular Birmingham-based lifestyle magazine *Southern Living*.

**Mobile Botanical Gardens**
5151 Museum Dr., Mobile, AL 36608
(251) 342-0555, MobileBotanicalGardens.org

**Huntsville Botanical Garden**
4747 Bob Wallace Ave. SW, Huntsville, AL 35805
(256) 830-4447, hsvbg.org

**Birmingham Botanical Garden**
2612 Lane Park Rd., Birmingham, AL 35223
(205) 414-3950, BBGardens.org

# SKI
## AT CLOUDMONT

Yes, really and truly, you can ski in Alabama. Cloudmont Ski Resort is the Southeastern-most ski resort in the country, located atop Lookout Mountain in the northeast corner of the state. As you might expect, the skiing season is relatively short, and man-made snow allows the resort to exist. Machines start creating the powdery white stuff when overnight temperatures fall to twenty-eight degrees or below. The snowpack is spread over two thousand-foot slopes, which rise 150 feet.

The site is perfect for beginning skiers. Cloudmont staff understand that Alabamians are more likely to own swimming trunks and hunting rifles than ski poles and snowboards, so all necessary equipment is available for rent. If your hopes of becoming the next gold-medal-winning winter Olympian evaporate in unseasonably warm weather, there are still plenty of fun excursions to experience, such as hiking and horseback riding at the resort's dude ranch.

721 County Rd. 614, Mentone, AL 35984
(256) 634-4344, Cloudmont.com

# HIKE
## TO THE WALLS OF JERICHO

Right along Alabama's border with Tennessee you'll find the Walls of Jericho, an impressive geological feature shaped by the waters of Turkey Creek carving through the limestone bedrock. As long as there's not a drought in the area, the creek forms a waterfall that flows into a bowl-shaped amphitheater with two-hundred-foot sheer rock walls.

Reaching the Walls of Jericho is not for the faint of heart or out of shape. You'll want to bring a snack or two and some water, as it takes about six hours to hike the 6.6-mile trail, which is rated difficult and descends more than a thousand feet. Along the way, you might catch sight of rare species of birds, such as the ruffed grouse, and wildlife, such as Alabama lamp mussels or the pale lilliput, which both live in Hurricane Creek. A narrow footbridge leads hikers over Hurricane Creek. The Walls of Jericho are at the midway point of the hike, making it a perfect place to catch your breath and enjoy the awe-inspiring views.

GPS coordinates for hiking trails parking lot: N 34.976624 W -86.080372
Scottsboro, AL
AlabamaForeverWild.com/walls-jericho

# MARVEL AT THE SIZE OF THE BIG OAK
## IN FOWLER PARK

There's something quintessentially Southern about live oak trees, with their craggy, tough bark and curling, expansive limbs. Seeing one makes you want to grab a glass of ice-cold lemonade or sweet tea and sit a spell in its shade. The Big Oak in Geneva's Robert Fowler Memorial Park is one of the state's largest live oaks, with a trunk that's twenty-two feet in diameter. Its branches spread out more than 163 feet. To put that into perspective, imagine you could clone retired NBA star Shaquille O'Neal twenty-two times. If you placed all those clones end to end, the tree would still be slightly wider than the Shaq clones are tall.

Also known as the Ole Oak Tree and the Constitution Oak, the two-hundred-year-old tree has been a landmark in Geneva since its founding in 1868. Records show it was a popular meeting place for the town's founders as the area was being developed.

Once you've enjoyed a rest underneath the tree's boughs, explore the rest of the park, which is located at the convergence of the Choctawhatchee and Pea rivers.

GPS coordinates: N 31.0286267, W -85.858469
Geneva, AL
(334) 684-2485, CityofGeneva.com/parks

# STOP AND SMELL THE ROSES
## AT PETALS FROM THE PAST

One glance at Petals from the Past is all you need to realize that this is not your average garden center or roadside flower stand. The old farmhouse-turned-gift-shop on the property is surrounded by beautifully landscaped gardens with every kind of flowering plant. The remainder of the farm's fourteen acres is a true gardener's paradise. Hundreds of varieties of rare, antique, and heirloom perennial flowers, roses, shrubs, herbs, vegetables, and fruit trees are available for purchase and await discovery around every corner.

The Powell family opened Petals from the Past in 1994 to share their love of gardening, and they've incorporated hands-on opportunities for customers. With the gardens surrounding the property, folks get to see the growing conditions certain plants require. The gift shop offers numerous resources for budding horticulturists, and the family hosts gardening workshops in the farm's educational building. Even brown thumbs can find the inspiration and gather the knowledge necessary to give gardening a go.

16034 County Rd., 29, Jemison, AL 35085
(205) 646-0069, PetalsFromThePast.com

# WADE INTO THE WATER
## SURROUNDED BY CAHABA LILIES

Alabama is one of three states where you can find the rare Cahaba lily. From early May to late June, the Cahaba River is blanketed in white and green as these spiky flowers bloom by the thousands in the shallow, rocky shoals near the town of West Blocton.

They're a beautiful canvas for a nature photographer, and no boat is required to get that perfect close-up with your macro lens. The water is shallow enough that all you have to do is take off your shoes, roll up your pants legs, and step on in, but if you prefer the safety of the shore, there are scenic overlooks along the river.

If you need a bigger dose of botany, West Blocton hosts the Cahaba Lily Festival on the third Saturday of May, which includes special presentations about the flower and chauffeured bus rides to the river.

Cahaba Lily Center, 1012 W. Main St., West Blocton, AL 35184
www.CahabaLily.com

**HEAR THE ROAR OF ENGINES** (page 55)

SEE THE SHRIMP BOATS DURING THE BLESSING OF THE FLEET (page 39)

**GO ON A PILGRIMAGE** (page 110)

**MAKE METAL ART AT SLOSS FURNACES** (page 154)

*Photo courtesy Matt Wilson*

**SPEND A DAY AT AN ART MUSEUM** (page 32)

**PICK A PEACH** (page 19)

*Photo courtesy Matt Wilson*

**ENJOY THE SCENERY AND THE SPREAD** (page 12)

FIND UNIQUE FOLK ART (page 130)

**PICK THE PERFECT PUMPKIN** (page 40)

**TAKE IN THE VIEW** (page 64)

**PEEL A SATSUMA** (page 23)

**THROW SHOES OVER THE LINE** (page 43)

**TASTE-TEST GOAT CHEESE** (page 20)

*Photo courtesy Morgan Graham*

Photo courtesy Jim Allen Simply Southern TV

**EXPERIENCE THE COURTROOM DRAMA**
*TO KILL A MOCKINGBIRD* (page 26)

# CULTURE AND HISTORY

# CROSS THE EDMUND PETTUS BRIDGE
## AND STROLL THROUGH OLD LIVE OAK CEMETERY

The city of Selma has a rich, complicated history. Settled in 1815, it quickly became a bustling river town thanks to the cotton industry. During the Civil War, its ironworks and shipbuilding facilities provided arms and equipment for the Confederacy, and on March 7, 1965, the city's Edmund Pettus Bridge was the site of "Bloody Sunday," when peaceful civil rights activists were met with violence during their march from Selma to Montgomery.

You'll cross the bridge driving into Selma on US Highway 80. Ironically, the iconic bridge of the civil rights movement is named for a former Confederate soldier and Ku Klux Klan grand wizard. Pettus is buried in the Old Live Oak Cemetery, and a stroll through this peaceful place, lined with Spanish moss-covered live oaks and magnolias, is a nice reminder that hatred isn't worth the effort. We're all going to end up six feet under. Prominent people buried at the cemetery include former US Vice President William Rufus King, military strategist William Hardee, and Benjamin Sterling Turner, Alabama's first African American congressman, who was elected in 1870.

Old Live Oak Cemetery 22 Dallas Ave., Selma, AL 36701

# EXPLORE THE GHOST TOWNS
## OF FORMER ALABAMA CAPITALS

Since Alabama became an official US territory in 1817, five cities have served as Alabama's capital. Tuscaloosa, Huntsville, and Montgomery (the current capital) are still thriving population centers, but that's not the case for the other former capitals.

It's been so long since anyone has lived in Cahawba, the state's first capital, that nowadays people can't even agree on how to spell the city's name. Some say it's Cahawba, while others say it's Cahaba, like the river. However you spell it, though, Cahawba and its handful of standing structures make for an interesting stop for lovers of history, archaeology, and ghost stories.

Remains are all that remain of St. Stephens, Alabama's territorial capital. It is now a recreational park and archaeological site, and a keen eye can pick out old home foundations of the once-bustling river town.

Old Cahawba, 9518 Cahaba Rd., Orrville, AL 36767
(334) 872-8058, Cahawba.com

St. Stephens Historical Park, 2056 Jim Long Rd., St. Stephens, AL 36569
(251) 247-2622, OldStStephens.net

# CONFRONT THE PAINFUL HISTORY
## OF LYNCHINGS IN AMERICA

History is filled with acts fueled by pure hatred—acts we wish we didn't have to remember because we truly wish they'd never happened and because they make us confront the painful truth that humanity is capable of atrocities. But we do remember them—to honor the memories of the guiltless victims and to hopefully avoid repeating those atrocities in the future.

In 2018, the National Memorial for Peace and Justice opened in Montgomery. It's the nation's first memorial dedicated to more than 4,400 African American men, women and children who were known to be killed by angry white mobs between 1877 and 1950. Eight hundred steel monuments hang from the rafters of the memorial, one for each county where a lynching occurred, inscribed with the names of the lynching victims. Sculptures and other memorials on the grounds focus on the injustices of slavery, Jim Crow laws, and modern-day presumptions of guilt in criminal investigations.

Visiting the memorial and its sister museum are powerful, emotional, heart-wrenching experiences. Give yourself ample time to ruminate and soak it all in.

**The National Memorial for Peace and Justice**
417 Caroline St., Montgomery, AL 36104

**The Legacy Museum**
115 Coosa St., Montgomery, AL 36104

**Ticket Office**
130 Commerce St., Montgomery, AL 36104

(334) 386-9100, MuseumAndMemorial.EJI.org

# CURL UP
## UNDER A GEE'S BEND QUILT

Each item created by the women of the Gee's Bend Quilters Collective tells a story of perseverance in not only the desire to capture the American Dream but also the even greater desire to be seen as equal citizens.

Gee's Bend is a rural community in Wilcox County, surrounded on three sides by the Alabama River and populated mostly by descendants of slaves. In 1962, residents took a fifteen-minute ferry ride into Camden, the county seat, and marched for their right to vote. Following the march, county leaders thwarted the civil rights efforts by suspending ferry service to Gee's Bend. It left residents isolated with only one way to get to town—a two-hour car ride.

The people of Gee's Bend were used to relying on their resourcefulness to make ends meet. The women started quilting bees and gained national acclaim for their artful quilt designs. In the following decades, the quilts of Gee's Bend were displayed in Houston's Museum of Fine Arts and the Whitney Museum of American Art in New York City. The women of Gee's Bend continue to create and sell their quilts today through the Gee's Bend Quilters Collective, which opened in 2003.

Gee's Bend Quilters Collective; call before visiting
14570 County Rd. 29, Boykin, AL 36723
(334) 573-2323, QuiltsofGeesBend.com

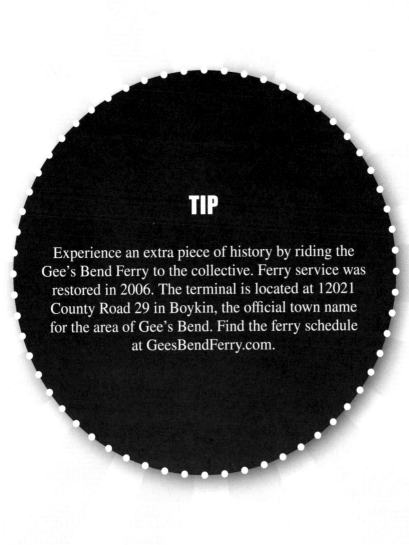

## TIP

Experience an extra piece of history by riding the
Gee's Bend Ferry to the collective. Ferry service was
restored in 2006. The terminal is located at 12021
County Road 29 in Boykin, the official town name
for the area of Gee's Bend. Find the ferry schedule
at GeesBendFerry.com.

# LEARN ABOUT LEADING LADIES
## AT THE ALABAMA
## WOMEN'S HALL OF FAME

Judson College was founded in 1838 as one of the nation's first institutions of higher education for women. The college continues operation today and is home to the Alabama Women's Hall of Fame. Vocations of inductees range from medicine and education to entertainment and civil rights. More than ninety bronze plaques hang from the walls of Howard Bean Hall, each depicting an Alabama woman and providing details on how she exemplified excellence. Portraits, letters, and other mementos from the women's lives are displayed in museum collections.

Inductees include names familiar to all Americans, such as Helen Keller, Coretta Scott King, and Rosa Parks. Others in the hall of fame left their mark in history without becoming household names, such as Julia Tutwiler, who championed education and prison reform, and Kathryn Tucker Windham, who entertained readers with Southern folktales and novels, including *13 Alabama Ghosts and Jeffrey*.

302 Bibb St., Marion, AL 36756
(334) 683-5167, awhf.org

## DID YOU KNOW?

Judson College has its own
china pattern, featuring campus buildings and
scenery. The china is manufactured in Staffordshire,
England, and can be purchased at the campus
bookstore, the Vault.

# EXPERIENCE THE HISTORY
## OF TUSKEGEE

Booker T. Washington was born into slavery in Virginia in 1856. After emancipation, he started school and graduated college. In 1881, life took him back to a plantation, albeit an abandoned one, in Tuskegee, Alabama, where he founded a college for African Americans that's now known as Tuskegee University.

In 1896, George Washington Carver joined Tuskegee's staff at Washington's request. During his forty-seven years as a professor, Carver became a renowned agricultural researcher, finding new uses for peanuts, sweet potatoes, and cowpeas. Both men are buried on the campus where they created lasting legacies that changed the lives of countless African Americans. That includes the Tuskegee Airmen, the first African American pilots in the US military who served during World War II, and the six founding members of the Grammy Award-winning funk and soul band the Commodores, who met as freshmen at Tuskegee.

In 1974, Tuskegee Institute was designated a National Historic Site, and it remains the only university campus in the nation with such a designation.

**George Washington Carver Museum**
1212 W. Montgomery Rd., Tuskegee, AL 36088
(334) 727-3200, nps.gov/tuin

**The Oaks—Booker T. Washington's home**
905 W. Montgomery Rd., Tuskegee, AL 36088
Find tour schedule and buy tickets at the George Washington
Carver Museum.

**Tuskegee Airmen National Historic Site**
1616 Chappie James Ave., Tuskegee, AL 36083
(334) 724-0922, nps.gov/tuai

**Commodores Museum**
208 E. Martin Luther King Hwy., Tuskegee, AL 36083
(334) 724-0777

**Tuskegee History Center**
104 S. Elm St., Tuskegee, AL 36083
(334) 724-0800, TuskegeeCenter.org

# LEARN NATIVE AMERICAN HISTORY
## IN MOUNDVILLE

Alabama teems with Native American history dating back thousands of years. In no place is that history more evident than Moundville Archaeological Park, just thirteen miles south of Tuscaloosa. In the 1300s, before European settlement, this was one of America's most populated cities north of present-day Mexico. Members of the Mississippian Indian civilization created a city here on three hundred acres of land that borders the Black Warrior River. They built twenty-nine earthen mounds used for civic and ceremonial purposes.

Adding to the site's interesting history, the Civilian Conservation Corps restored the mounds and built a museum in the 1930s to preserve and present the rich Native American history of Moundville. Most recently, the Jones Archaeological Museum reopened in 2010 after renovations to incorporate new technology into exhibits. The park hosts its annual Native American Festival in October, but visitors are welcome to explore the park and its nature trails any day of the week.

634 Mound State Pkwy., Moundville, AL 35474
(205) 371-2234, moundville.museums.ua.edu

# LOOK AROUND THE ALICEVILLE MUSEUM
## FOR WWII HISTORY ✓

American soldiers traveled to distant shores to fight in World War II. But oceans away from the war frontier, the tiny town of Aliceville had its own role. From 1943 to 1945, more than six thousand German soldiers were held in a prisoner of war (POW) camp built in the city. They were part of the famous Afrika Korps, led by German marshal Erwin Rommel. The prisoners were treated well, following rules set forth in the Geneva Convention. They were paid eighty cents a day for labor, received healthcare, and were fed at least three times a day.

Once Germany surrendered in 1945, the prisoners were sent back to their home countries, and the camp was dismantled. But the city has preserved memories of its role in World War II. The Aliceville Museum includes a permanent exhibit of POW artifacts, the largest of its kind in the country. Its multimedia displays include video interviews of former POWs and camp personnel.

104 Broad St. NE, Aliceville, AL 35442
(205) 373-2363, AlicevilleMuseum.org

### DID YOU KNOW?
Aliceville was Alabama's largest POW camp during WWII, but thousands of German prisoners were also held at camps in Fort McClellan, Fort Rucker, and Opelika.

# GO ON A PILGRIMAGE
## TO ANTEBELLUM HOMES

Some of Alabama's greatest treasures are its remaining antebellum mansions. While you can find handfuls of these stately manors in Huntsville, Montgomery, and Mobile, others require a lengthy jaunt driving county roads through the rural countryside. Traveling through such scenic surroundings sets the mood as a reminder of a time when life moved a bit slower, and while travelers can take a driving tour of historic homes any time of the year, those with the heart of Scarlett O'Hara will be satisfied only after going on a pilgrimage to tour the mansions.

Two of the largest—the Selma Pilgrimage and the Eufaula Pilgrimage—occur in the spring. In Eufaula, Shorter Mansion is a can't-miss. The home was featured in the movie *Sweet Home Alabama*. In Selma, the charred floor of the Kenan Plantation, built in 1826, shows that Union troops tried to destroy the home. The city of Eutaw (pronounced like the state of Utah) hosts its annual pilgrimage in October. While participating homes rotate, the Kirkwood mansion is Eutaw's must-see. It was built in 1858, and visitors must climb three flights of stairs to reach the cupola.

**Towns for driving tours:**
Athens, Camden, Lowndesboro, Greensboro,
Demopolis, Marion, Livingston

**Selma Pilgrimage Ticket Office**
**Vaughan-Smitherman Museum**
109 Union St., Selma, AL 36701
(334) 412-8550, SelmaPilgrimage.org

**Eufaula Pilgrimage Ticket Office**
**First Presbyterian Church Fellowship Hall**
201 N. Randolph Ave., Eufaula, AL 36027
(334) 687-3793, EufaulaPilgrimage.com

**Eutaw Pilgrimage Ticket Office, Vaughn-Morrow House**
310 Main St., Eutaw, AL 35462
(205) 292-0015, greenecountyhistoricsociety.org/GCHS/
Annual_Tour.html

# MEANDER THROUGH
## THE MUSEUM OF ALABAMA

The Museum of Alabama tells the history of the Union's twenty-second state through three permanent exhibitions. The Land of Alabama focuses on the state's unique and plentiful natural resources. More than fourteen thousand years of Native American history is presented in the First Alabamians exhibition, but the museum's centerpiece is its newest exhibit, Alabama Voices.

Opened in 2014, the state-of-the-art Alabama Voices exhibit is a history buff's dream, winding through beautiful displays and dioramas with more than eight hundred artifacts dating from 1700 to the present day. Twenty-two audiovisual recordings, which include the words of former slaves and soldiers from the Civil War and two world wars, add a moving living-history element to the tour.

The museum is housed in the Alabama Department of Archives and History, the nation's oldest state-funded, independent, and historical agency. Built between 1938 and 1940 as one of the last New Deal-funded projects, the department now boasts a catalog of more than a half million artifacts.

624 Washington Ave., Montgomery, AL 36130
(334) 242-4435, Museum.Alabama.gov

# MEET "ALABAMA'S FIRST FAMILY"
## AT THE BANKHEAD HOUSE

In 1940, President Franklin Delano Roosevelt and future president Harry S. Truman joined nearly thirty thousand spectators in Jasper, Alabama, for the funeral of William Brockman Bankhead. A member of "Alabama's First Family," Bankhead served eleven terms in the US House of Representatives and was speaker of the House at the time of his death. His leadership was integral in passing the Fair Labor Standards Act, which established a forty-hour work week and abolished child labor.

Bankhead's contributions are memorialized in the library of the Bankhead Home and Heritage Center. He had the colonial-revival home built in 1925, and it was restored in 2010. The library also pays tribute to the congressional service of six other Walker County men, including Bankhead's father, brother, and nephew.

Another room in the home is dedicated to Bankhead's daughter, actress Tallulah. She amassed more than three hundred acting credits on stage and in film and TV, including lead actress in Alfred Hitchcock's *Lifeboat*. She was known for her husky voice and catchphrase, "Hello, dahling."

800 Seventh St. W. Jasper, AL 35501
(205) 302-0001, bhandhc.org

# HIKE TO THE FURNACES
## AT TANNEHILL IRONWORKS

In the early 1860s, three imposing stone blast furnaces at Tannehill Ironworks churned out twenty-two tons of pig iron daily to help power the Confederate war machine, but those furnaces abruptly stopped production in March 1865 when Union troops heavily damaged the production facilities during Wilson's Raid. The structures themselves, though, have been preserved and are the cornerstones of the 1,500-acre Tannehill Ironworks Historical State Park, one of Alabama's twenty-two sites on the Civil War Discovery Trail.

To better appreciate a tour of the furnaces, you may want to brush up on your industrial history with a stroll through the park's Iron and Steel Museum of Alabama. Pick up a map at the visitor center because the furnaces are a short hike off the road. Plus, the map will point you toward the park's other attractions, including a grist mill, an old cemetery, restored pioneer cabins, hiking and biking trails, fishing areas, and campsites.

12632 Confederate Pkwy., McCalla, AL 35111
(205) 477-5711, Tannehill.org

## TIP

For another uniquely Alabama experience, visit during a monthly Trade Day. More than four hundred vendors set up shop for an outdoor flea market. Plus, talented artisans, including a potter, quilter, painter, blacksmith, and engraver, ply their trades in restored pioneer cabins on the property.

# REMINISCE WITH A SPANISH-AMERICAN WAR HERO
## AT MAGNOLIA GROVE

Magnolia Grove in Greensboro is the quintessential old plantation mansion. Built in 1835, the white Greek Revival facade impresses with six massive Doric columns. It's where Rear Admiral Richmond Pearson Hobson was reared.

Hobson fought in the Spanish-American War and became a national hero when he led a mission to sink the USS *Merrimac* in an attempt to trap the Spanish fleet. While unsuccessful, Hobson and his men survived and were awarded the Congressional Medal of Honor by President Franklin Delano Roosevelt. After his naval career, Hobson served as a US representative from Alabama for nearly a decade and was a champion of Prohibition.

Magnolia Grove houses numerous treasures, including the sign from the USS *Merrimac*. Behind the home stand old slaves' quarters and an original two-story building, which housed the kitchen, laundry, and servants' quarters. Plus, a portion of the plantation's original boxwood gardens also remains.

1002 Hobson St., Greensboro, AL 36744
(334) 624-8618
ahc.alabama.gov/properties/magnoliagrove/magnoliagrove.aspx

# SIP TEA
## WITH MARTHA WASHINGTON

History comes alive at American Village in Montevallo. Strolling across the grounds, you're likely to come across a boisterous group of colonists led by Patrick Henry protesting the Stamp Act or General George Washington's Continental Army as the soldiers practice marching in formation across the green. Inside the replica of Mount Vernon, Martha Washington and Abigail Adams enjoy hosting tea parties while teaching about manners, appropriate dress, and dancing. With twenty colonial-inspired buildings across 180 acres, a visit to American Village will reinvigorate your patriotism through all the lively reenactments.

American Village is open year-round, but visiting during one of its seasonal programs adds another level to your experience. The site hosts the Festival of Tulips in the spring, a special Independence Day celebration on, of course, July 4, the Liberty Experience in the fall, and Christmas luncheons and tours during the winter.

3727 Hwy. 119, Montevallo, AL 35115
(205) 665-3535, AmericanVillage.org

# WALK THROUGH HISTORY
## ON MONTGOMERY'S DEXTER AVENUE

You'd be hard-pressed to find another street that encompasses so much complicated history in just half a mile. Dexter Avenue starts at the town square, where Montgomery's slave markets once stood. It's where a work-wearied Rosa Parks boarded a bus for a ride that would spark the Montgomery Bus Boycott…where the Confederate Secretary of War sent the telegram that ordered troops to fire on Fort Sumter, starting the Civil War…and where a young Martin Luther King Jr. pastored his first church.

The State Capitol at the end of the street is where Jefferson Davis was sworn in as president of the Confederacy and where one hundred years later King addressed a crowd of thousands to end a five-day, fifty-four-mile march from Selma to Montgomery to bring attention to the need for federal voting rights legislation protecting African American voters. Make Dexter Avenue your first step in exploring the sites on the US Civil Rights Trail in Montgomery.

**Alabama State Capitol**
600 Dexter Ave., Montgomery, AL 36104

**Dexter Avenue King Memorial Baptist Church**
454 Dexter Ave., Montgomery, AL 36104
(334) 356-3494, DexterKingMemorial.org

**Dexter Parsonage Museum**
309 S. Jackson St., Montgomery, AL 36104
(334) 261-3270, DexterKingMemorial.org

**Rosa Parks Museum**
252 Montgomery St., Montgomery, AL 36104
(334) 241-8615, troy.edu/student-life-resources/arts-culture/rosa-parks-museum/index.html

**Freedom Rides Museum**
210 S. Court St., Montgomery, AL 36104
(334) 414-8647, ahc.alabama.gov/properties/freedomrides/freedomrides.aspx

# STEP ABOARD
## THE USS *ALABAMA*

The USS *Alabama* battleship saw action in the Pacific Theater during World War II starting in 1943 and was decommissioned in 1947. The 680-foot, 45,000-ton "Mighty A" earned nine battle stars during its five years of service. By 1964, the stately ship seemed destined for the scrap heap, but forward-thinking Alabama citizens devised a campaign to save her and make her the cornerstone of a park dedicated to honoring veterans of all branches of military service.

Today the battleship rests in Mobile Bay as an imposing but welcoming sight to visitors of the 155-acre USS Alabama Battleship Memorial Park. Since opening in 1965, the park has become one of the state's most successful attractions, with hundreds of thousands of tourists stepping aboard the ship every year. Guests may choose from three tours of the battleship, ranging in length from one hour to an entire day, but there's plenty more to see at the park, including memorials, tanks, artillery, a military aircraft pavilion, and the USS *Drum*, a World War II submarine.

2703 Battleship Pkwy., Mobile, AL 36602
(251) 433-2703, USSAlabama.com

# STEP FOOT
## IN ALABAMA'S ONLY FRANK LLOYD WRIGHT HOUSE

Legendary American architect Frank Lloyd Wright designed more than one thousand buildings in cities across the globe, including the Guggenheim Museum in New York City, the Imperial Hotel in Tokyo, and the Fallingwater home in Pennsylvania, but he also left his mark in Alabama. In 1940, Wright designed a home for Florence residents Stanley and Mildred Rosenbaum following his Usonian concept, a space- and cost-efficient design.

Keeping with Wright's style of organic architecture, the L-shaped home's bricks and cypress trees melt into the surrounding landscape. Plentiful windows allow the sun to heat the home in the winter, while numerous overhangs block out the sun's heat during the summer. Although Wright thought window and porch screens were tacky, they play an important role in a Southern home—keeping insects at bay year-round.

Stanley Rosenbaum passed away in 1983, but Mildred remained in the home before selling it to the city of Florence in 1999. It was renovated and opened as a museum in 2002. It is the only Wright home in the South that's open to the public.

601 Riverview Dr., Florence, AL 35630
(256) 718-5050, WrightInAlabama.com

# PAY YOUR RESPECTS
## AT A NATIONAL CEMETERY

It takes courage, patriotism, and selflessness to serve in the US armed forces. Alabama is home to three national cemeteries that provide worthy resting places for these brave men and women and their families. While the cemetery settings are peaceful and serene, the rows of white marble headstones serve as a reminder that American freedom is a great privilege—one that is only possible thanks to their sacrifices.

The oldest of the three, the Mobile National Cemetery, was established in 1865 after the city fell to the Union in the Civil War. More than six hundred Union soldiers are buried there along with a number of Apache Indians, including relatives of the great Apache leader Geronimo. It's also the final resting place for John Dury New, who received the Medal of Honor for his service during World War II. Matthew Leonard, a Medal of Honor recipient who fought in the Korean War and died in the Vietnam War, is buried at Fort Mitchell National Cemetery. The newest of the three cemeteries, the Alabama National Cemetery in Montevallo, opened in 2009.

**Mobile National Cemetery**
1202 Virginia St., Mobile, AL 36604
(850) 453-4846, cem.va.gov/cems/nchp/mobile.asp

**Fort Mitchell National Cemetery**
553 Hwy. 165, Ft. Mitchell, AL 36856
(334) 855-4731, cem.va.gov/cems/nchp/ftmitchell.asp

**Alabama National Cemetery**
3133 Hwy. 119, Montevallo, AL 35115
(205) 665-9039, cem.va.gov/cems/nchp/alabama.asp

# TOUCH THE WATER PUMP
## AT IVY GREEN

The 1962 film *The Miracle Worker* forever etched a scene in the collective memories of generations of Americans—the moment when a frustrated and angry seven-year-old, who had been blind, deaf, and mute most of her life, finally learned to communicate thanks to her dedicated teacher and a water pump. The movie was based on the real-life story of Helen Keller and her teacher, Anne Sullivan. While the cinematic scene may seem dramatized for Hollywood, that interaction really took place in Tuscumbia, Alabama, at Keller's childhood home, Ivy Green.

In 1954, the home was placed on the National Register of Historic Places. The house and grounds, including the water pump, are preserved as a tribute to the miraculous life of Keller, who went on to become a prolific writer, noted speaker, and activist for the blind and deaf. The home is open for tours year-round, but for a special treat, plan your trip in June or July to catch the locals performing the *Miracle Worker* play on the grounds.

300 N. Commons St. W., Tuscumbia, AL 35674
(256) 383-4066, HelenKellerBirthplace.org

# SEE WHERE ANDREW JACKSON BECAME A HERO
## AT HORSESHOE BEND

Without the battle of Horseshoe Bend, the United States may never have known Andrew Jackson as its seventh president. Before he was promoted to major general and before the Battle of New Orleans, General Jackson successfully led US troops against a group of Creek Indians in the Battle of Horseshoe Bend, named for a curve in the Tallapoosa River. It was effectively the final battle of the Creek War of 1813–14. Five months later, the Creeks signed a treaty and ceded twenty-three million acres of land, including the area that became the state of Alabama.

The site has been preserved and is run by the National Park Service. Guided tours are available but must be scheduled in advance. During daylight hours, visitors can drive a solemn three-mile tour around the edge of the battlefield or hike a 2.8-mile trail. Keep a keen eye out for numerous unique bird species. The site is part of the Piedmont Plateau Birding Trail, but if you prefer boats to birds, there is the Miller Bridge Boat Ramp, where you can put into the Tallapoosa River.

11288 Horseshoe Bend Rd., Daviston, AL 36256
(256) 234-7111, nps.gov/hobe

# TOUR
## ALABAMA CONSTITUTION HALL

On July 5, 1819, when the American flag had only twenty-one stars, forty-four delegates started holding meetings in a cabinet shop in Huntsville to begin the process of turning Alabama from a territory into a state. They completed their work on December 14, 1819, when Alabama was admitted to the Union.

The original cabinet shop and surrounding buildings were lost to history, but in 1968 a dedicated group of local historians discovered the old buildings' foundations through excavations and set about constructing replicas. What's now known as Alabama Constitution Hall Historic Park & Museum opened to the public in 1982 and reopened in 2019 after undergoing renovations in preparation for the state's bicentennial. Along with the cabinet shop, the grounds include a print shop, law office, federal land surveyor's office, post office, and the former residence of Sheriff Stephen Neal. Tourists can walk through the grounds or plan a trip to the museum during one of its living-history events.

109 Gates Ave., Huntsville, AL 35801
(256) 564-8100, EarlyWorks.com/alabama-constitution-hall-park

## DID YOU KNOW?

The hall is one of three museums in the EarlyWorks
Family of Museums along with the EarlyWorks
Children's Museum and the Huntsville Depot and
Museum in historic Huntsville. Make a day of it
and visit all three!

# RIDE THE MOBILE BAY FERRY
## FROM ONE HISTORIC FORT TO ANOTHER

The entrance to Mobile Bay was once protected by two land fortresses: Fort Morgan on the east and Fort Gaines on the west. While both functioned during World War I and World War II, the forts most famously came under direct fire during the Civil War in the Battle of Mobile Bay. A Confederate torpedo sank the Union's USS *Tecumseh* during the battle, which reportedly led Union admiral David Farragut to shout his immortal words, "Damn the torpedoes, full speed ahead!" By August 23, 1865, both forts had fallen to the Union.

Fort Morgan and Fort Gaines now operate as historical sites, offering a look back at American coastal defenses. A drive between the two forts, on land, would take more than two hours, and that's only if there's no beach traffic to contend with. Thankfully, a scenic forty-minute ride on the Mobile Bay Ferry takes motorists and pedestrians alike directly from one fort to the other.

**Fort Morgan**
110 Hwy. 180, Gulf Shores, AL 36542
(251) 540-7127, Fort-Morgan.org

**Fort Gaines**
51 Bienville Blvd., Dauphin Island, AL 36528
(251) 861-6992, DauphinIsland.org/Fort-Gaines

**Mobile Bay Ferry**
SR 193 on Dauphin Island (Fort Gaines side)
and SR 180 on Mobile Point (Fort Morgan side)
(251) 861-3000, MobileBayFerry.com

# FIND UNIQUE FOLK ART
## AT KENTUCK

Back in the 1800s, the city of Northport was simply a settlement known as Kentuck, which means "a heaven kind of place." The Kentuck Art Center in downtown Northport retains this historic name and certainly feels like heaven for any art aficionado. The impressive artwork starts on the outside, with the proud, red-coated pointer sculpture sitting atop one of the center's five buildings. Just don't call him Clifford. This dog's name is Rusty, and he beckons visitors to stroll through the artists' studios, galleries, and collections.

Inside you'll discover a treasure trove of unique pieces, ranging from paintings, pottery, and sculptures to quilts, jewelry, and blown glass. The roots of Kentuck art are in folklife, with self-taught artists who create artwork from the materials that surround them.

For an extra-special experience, plan your trip to Northport in October for the two-day Kentuck Festival of the Arts, with 270 presenting artists, children's activities, concerts, and a spoken word stage.

503 Main Ave., Northport, AL 35476
(205) 758-1257, Kentuck.org

# RELISH THE CULTURE
## OF BLACK BELT TREASURES

Alabama's Black Belt region forms a band of nineteen counties across the center of the state. The area's rich, black topsoil attracted settlers in the early 1800s who were looking to make a profit in the cotton industry. By the time of the Civil War, most of the state's slaves lived in this region, and after the conflict many freedmen remained in the area, working as sharecroppers.

Thanks to the unique melding of African American and Anglo-Saxon influences, the Black Belt developed its own culture. Economically depressed but strong in spirit, the resourceful, resilient, and quick-witted people of the Black Belt found artistic forms of expression using available materials. Those talents are on display in every nook and cranny of the Black Belt Treasures Cultural Arts Center. The pottery, quilts, crafts, books, jewelry, and paintings available for purchase were all created by Black Belt artists, and if you time it right, you could learn to create your own Black Belt-inspired art during one of the center's many workshops.

209 Claiborne St., Camden, AL 36726
(334) 682-9878, BlackBeltTreasures.com

# SEE THE WORLD IN MINIATURE
## AT AVE MARIA GROTTO

Brother Joseph was a miniature man, weighing about a hundred pounds and standing around five feet tall, thanks to an accident that left him slightly hunchbacked. Born in Bavaria, Brother Joseph moved to Alabama in 1892 at the age of fourteen to live in the state's only Benedictine abbey for men. His job at the abbey was shoveling coal at the powerhouse.

This diminutive man discovered that he was very talented at creating realistic replicas of holy and historic places from mere stone and cement embedded with discarded items, such as broken plates or old jewelry. From religious sites, such as St. Peter's Basilica and Calvary, to historic places, including the Coliseum and the Leaning Tower of Pisa, Brother Joseph created his sculptures by hand based on photographs or written descriptions. During his nearly seventy years at St. Bernard Abbey, Brother Joseph created more than 125 structures in miniature. He died in 1961, but all his works remain in the abbey's Ave Maria Grotto, visited by thousands annually.

1600 St. Bernard Dr. SE, Cullman, AL 35055
(256) 734-4110, AveMariaGrotto.com

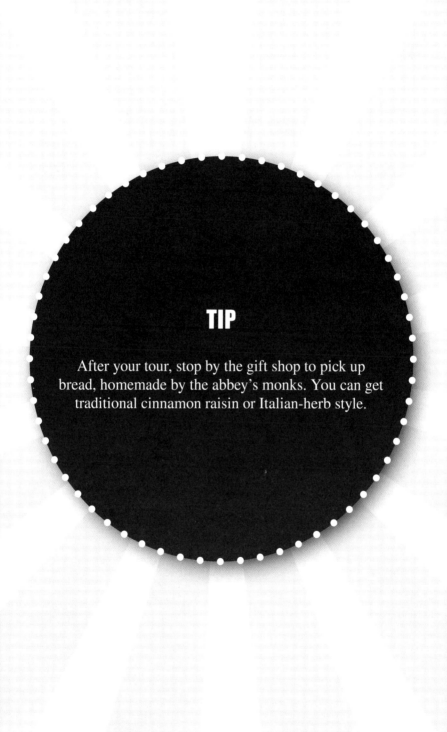

## TIP

After your tour, stop by the gift shop to pick up bread, homemade by the abbey's monks. You can get traditional cinnamon raisin or Italian-herb style.

# STUDY
## THE STATE'S FOSSIL RECORD

It's been said that Alabama is the best place in the United States to search for fossils east of the Mississippi River. Archaeologists have found everything from plant and mollusk fossils to vertebrates and dinosaur bones within the state's borders. Alabama even has an official state fossil—the *Basilosaurus cetoides*, an ancient toothed whale. Plus, the *Appalachiosaurus montgomeriensis*, a type of tyrannosaur related to the T-rex, is only known to be found in Alabama.

To really appreciate the diversity and scope of the state's fossil record, visit any of these museums. Or head to Shark Tooth Creek to find your own fossil keepsake. In prehistoric times, the creek was part of a barrier island. Today, whenever it rains, ancient shark teeth are dislodged from the surrounding soil and can be easily found along the creek bank.

## McWane Science Center
View the most complete Appalachiosaurus skeleton
ever discovered, along with other dinosaur bones.
200 Nineteenth St. N., Birmingham, AL 35203
(205) 714-8300, McWane.org

## Alabama Museum of Natural History
See the state's official fossil. As a bonus, the museum
also houses the Hodges Meteorite, the only meteorite that's
known to have hit a human. Sylacauga native Ann Elizabeth
Fowler Hodges was injured in the strike.
427 Sixth Ave., Tuscaloosa, AL 35487
(205) 348-7500, almnh.museums.ua.edu

## Auburn University Museum of Natural History
Houses the only dinosaur egg found in US
soil east of the Mississippi River.
381 Mell St., Auburn, AL 36849
(334) 844-9127, aumnh.org

## Anniston Museum of Natural History
Its Dynamic Earth exhibit includes bones and life-sized casts
of dinosaurs. As a bonus, visit the Berman Museum next door for
the intriguing story of two World War II spies. They spied
on each other, fell in love, married after the war, and lived in
Anniston until their deaths.
800 Museum Dr., Anniston, AL 36206
(256) 237-6766, exploreamag.org

## Shark Tooth Creek
Visitors are allowed to take home up to ten shark teeth.
Tours by appointment only.
24114 Alabama Hwy. 14 E., Aliceville, AL 35442
(205) 373-2605, SharkToothCreek.com

# FIND HISTORY PRESERVED
## AT OLD ALABAMA TOWN

Most urban downtown centers are a hodgepodge of architectural designs, with federal and colonial-style buildings alongside Victorian-inspired train depots and mid-century modern offices. Alabama's capital city is no exception, that is, except for Old Alabama Town, which encompasses six city blocks in downtown Montgomery.

The attraction welcomes more than sixty thousand visitors annually, who tour its fifty authentically restored buildings and homes from the nineteenth century, including a grocery store, a one-room schoolhouse, a church, a cotton gin, and a print shop. Lucas Tavern, where the Marquis de Lafayette once stayed, is the oldest building in the collection. The antebellum Ordeman-Mitchell-Shaw House serves as the cornerstone of Old Alabama Town. The home was built in the 1850s, and its first residents were planters who used it as a townhome when they needed to stay in Montgomery. On daily guided tours, you'll see the townhome, the original slave quarters and kitchen, laundry facilities, storage rooms, and stable. You can also explore the entire grounds on a self-guided tour.

301 Columbus St., Montgomery, AL 36104
(334) 240-4500, LandmarksFoundation.com

*Photo courtesy Morgan Graham*

U.S. Space & Rocket Center

# UNIQUE ATTRACTIONS

# MEET THE LIONS
## AT THE UNIVERSITY OF NORTH
## ALABAMA

The president of the University of North Alabama (UNA) has some interesting neighbors—two Nubian lions. Thankfully, the lioness, Una, and lion, Leo III, are housed in a state-of-the-art, secure habitat beside the president's home. They also stay happily full, feasting on twelve pounds of meat daily, which surely helps the president sleep more comfortably at night.

The university was established in 1830, and its first live lion mascot came to the campus in 1974 and lived in the president's garage until a proper habitat could be built. Named Leo I, he famously nipped Miss Alabama's hindside during a photoshoot. When he passed away in 1988, the school quickly adopted Leo II, who saw UNA's football team win three straight Division II national championships starting in 1993. Una, pronounced "yoo-nah," became the first lioness mascot at the school when she joined her twin brother, Leo III, for the trip to Florence in 2003. While the university has a dedicated lion cam, it's no comparison to seeing these majestic beasts in person.

George H. Carroll Lion Habitat, Florence, AL 35630
256-765-4100, una.edu/lioncam

# CLAIM A GREAT DEAL
## AT UNCLAIMED BAGGAGE

Lost luggage and misplaced personal items are an unfortunate reality of air travel. When lost-and-found items are left unfound or when a suitcase is orphaned at an airport, those pieces start another journey to the Unclaimed Baggage Center store in Scottsboro, the only lost luggage store in the United States.

At the store's processing facility, workers receive the lost items, sort through the suitcases, remove trash, and categorize items for donations or retail sale. From there, the staff launders clothes, cleans fine jewelry, and tests electronics while wiping clean any personal data. Then, it's off to the sales floor, where customers can claim great deals on unclaimed baggage.

The store has been a family-run business since 1970, and workers have received and screened some interesting, unique, and flat-out weird items, including a full suit of armor, a 40.95-carat natural emerald, a camera from a space shuttle, and a mummified hawk.

509 W. Willow St., Scottsboro, AL 35768
(256) 259-1525, UnclaimedBaggage.com

### TIP
At 2:30 p.m. Monday through Saturday, you can watch "The Baggage Experience," where a staff member unpacks and sorts a newly received unclaimed bag.

# POSE WITH A PEANUT
## IN DOTHAN

Within a hundred miles of Dothan, Alabama, farmers grow nearly half the peanuts produced annually in the United States. In 2001, the city's downtown redevelopment group paid tribute to everyone's favorite legume with painted four-foot-tall peanut statues sold to and placed in front of area businesses. Today, the community art project and fund-raiser includes more than forty peanut statues scattered around town, which makes for a fun scavenger hunt for any peanut gallery.

The best place to start a tour of peanuts is at the Dothan Area Convention and Visitors Bureau. Along with maps of statue locations, the bureau houses a peanut painted like Elvis Presley, who was known to enjoy a good peanut butter and banana sandwich every now and again. After posing for a picture with the King, go nuts finding other fanciful peanuts, including the fire hydrant and dalmatian, superhero, TV director, and servicemen . . . or, service peanuts.

3311 Ross Clark Cir., Dothan, AL 36303
(334) 794-6622, VisitDothan.com

# TAKE A SELFIE
## WITH A MONUMENTAL INSECT

The Boll Weevil Monument built in 1919 is the world's first and perhaps only monument dedicated to an insect, and you'll find it in downtown Enterprise. It serves as a reminder of human ingenuity and perseverance during tough times.

In the 1800s, cotton was king in Alabama, but that started to change in 1915 thanks to the encroachment of the boll weevil. The voracious pests decimated cotton crops throughout the state, leaving farmers with empty fields and emptier wallets. To make a living, farmers in and around Enterprise started planting a new crop—peanuts. It took just one harvest for farmers to see a profit, and the landscape of Southeast Alabama was forever changed.

To this day, the area produces 50 percent of the nation's peanut crop, and it's all thanks to the insatiable insect depicted in the Boll Weevil Monument.

Intersection of College Street and Main Street, Enterprise, AL 36330

# ENCOUNTER EXOTIC ANIMALS
## AT ALABAMA GULF COAST ZOO

Zoos are perfect places to view exotic animals from faraway lands, but at the Alabama Gulf Coast Zoo, visitors venture behind the cages for up-close, personal encounters with the zoo's denizens. Laugh at the lemurs' hijinks and cuddle with a lynx. Meet a kangaroo and hang out with a sloth or two. Give an anteater a meal and learn about a reptile's appeal.

For safety's sake, encounters with the zoo's docile animals are supervised by experienced zookeepers. Aside from the zoo's gentlest creatures, other exhibits feature tigers, bears, leopards, birds, camels, and more. In total, Alabama Gulf Coast Zoo is home to six hundred animals, including twenty-two endangered species.

On top of all that, the zoo is the first to have to evacuate all its animals because of a hurricane. Animal Planet even retold the story of the zoo's 2005 evacuation caused by Hurricane Ivan in the documentary *The Little Zoo That Could*.

1204 Gulf Shores Pkwy., Gulf Shores, AL 36542
(251) 968-5783, AlabamaGulfCoastZoo.com

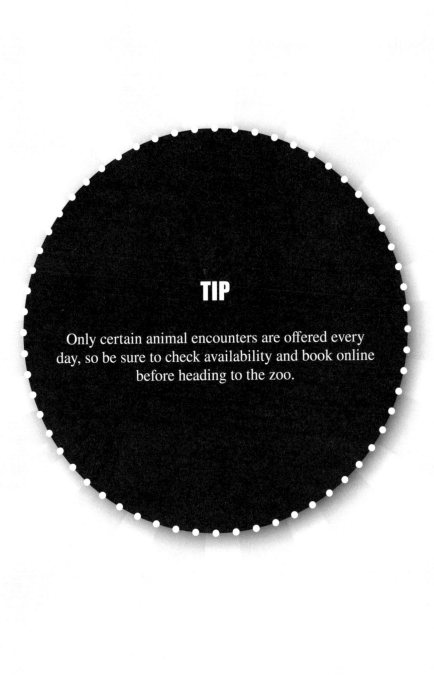

## TIP

Only certain animal encounters are offered every day, so be sure to check availability and book online before heading to the zoo.

# BREAK OUT
## OF THE OLD HOUSTON JAIL

Houston is an unincorporated community in Winston County, nicknamed the "Free State of Winston" for the prevalence of Union support during the Civil War. Once a bustling city, Houston served as county seat from 1858 to 1884, which required civic buildings, including a jail. Built in 1868 of native timber logs, the jail is the only structure remaining from the city's glory days.

The two-room building is believed to be the second-oldest wooden jail in the country. As a high-security feature, the wooden walls are peppered with thousands of horseshoe nails to discourage ruffians from sawing their way to freedom. With no indoor plumbing, a large hole drilled in the back wall served as the inmates' bathroom.

In the 2000s, local citizens led an effort to restore the jail, which was rededicated in 2008. Visitors from forty-eight states and more than twenty countries have toured the site, which is open year-round. During business hours, you can also see artifacts discovered during the restoration on display at the post office next door.

4806 County Rd. 63, Houston, AL 35572
soloso.com/Houston

# COUNT DOWN
## TO TAKEOFF
### AT THE US SPACE AND ROCKET CENTER

The US Space and Rocket Center in Huntsville is the official visitors center for NASA's Marshall Space Flight Center, which developed rockets, propulsion systems, and modules for the nation's first satellite, the Apollo missions to the moon, and the International Space Station.

Choosing the top options for what to see and do at the center feels as overwhelming as attempting to count the stars themselves. From rotating, world-class museum exhibits and the state-of-the-art planetarium to the immersive National Geographic theater and outer space simulator rides, no two visits to the US Space and Rocket Center will be the same, but don't miss the Saturn V Hall guided tour to see the authentic Saturn V rocket. This tribute to human ingenuity propelled mankind to the moon.

Add an eccentric stop to the trip by searching for the grave of Miss Baker, a squirrel monkey and the first US animal to successfully travel to space and back. The gravestone stands outside the center's main entrance in a grove of trees next to the parking lot.

1 Tranquility Base, Huntsville, AL 35805
(800) 637-7223, RocketCenter.com

# VISIT A RESTING PLACE
## FOR MAN'S BEST FRIEND

Small-game hunters are rugged—brawnier than the Brawny Man himself. Emotions rarely get the best of them, but when a hunter has to say goodbye to his trusty coonhound, all that machismo goes out the window.

That's the reality Key Underwood faced back in 1937 when his faithful companion and hunting dog of fifteen years, Troop, passed away. Sure, all dogs go to heaven, but Underwood wanted to make sure that Troop's final resting place on earth was worthy of man's best friend. He buried Troop at one of his favorite spots, a popular hunting camp in Colbert County. Other hunters followed suit.

Today, the Key Underwood Coon Dog Memorial Graveyard is the final resting place for more than 185 authentic coon dogs. It's the only cemetery of its kind in the world. Each Labor Day locals celebrate these hounds with Decoration Day, but visitors are welcome anytime.

4945 Coondog Cemetery Rd., Cherokee, AL 35616
(256) 412-5970, CoonDogCemetery.com

# EXAMINE
## THE WETUMPKA IMPACT CRATER

The landscape on the east side of the city of Wetumpka in Central Alabama bears scars of a massive impact scientists believe happened around eighty-five million years ago. In the late 1990s, a group of geologists proved the area's craggy hills were caused by a meteor strike, making this one of about thirty confirmed impact craters in the United States. Scientists believe the meteor was about the size of a football stadium when it struck the earth, traveling between ten and twenty miles per second and destroying all plant and animal life within a forty-mile radius.

Even after millions of years, the crater walls that create the circumference of the four-mile-wide impact zone remain prominent and can be viewed from numerous spots around town, including from Jasmine Hill Gardens as well as US Highway 231 as you drive in from Montgomery and from Harrogate Springs Road, about a mile east of the intersection with Jasmine Hill Road. It should be noted that most of the crater area is privately owned. For a more in-depth overview of the crater, the city of Wetumpka offers annual tours in late February or early March.

WetumpkaImpactCraterCommission.org

# WALK THE PATH
## ALONG THE WICHAHPI COMMEMORATIVE WALL

As a young woman of the Yuchi Indian tribe, Te-lah-nay was forcibly removed from her home in Northwest Alabama along what's now known as the Tennessee River during the Trail of Tears. Displaced to Oklahoma, she listened for rivers that sang as her people believed the Tennessee did. Finding none, she bravely walked back to her Alabama home, a journey that took her five years.

Te-lah-nay's story lived in family folklore until her great-great-grandson, Tom Hendrix, had her journals translated. To honor her determination in searching for the singing river, Hendrix spent thirty years building a rock wall. Composed of more than 8.5 million pounds of rocks gathered from all fifty states and 127 countries, the Wichahpi Commemorative Wall is the nation's largest unmortared rock wall. It varies in height and width, signifying the highs and lows Te-lah-nay experienced on her five-year journey. The wall is a moving, spiritual tribute to one family's dedication to finding your true home.

13890 County Rd. 8, Florence, AL 35633
(256) 764-3617, IfTheLegendsFade.com/author.html

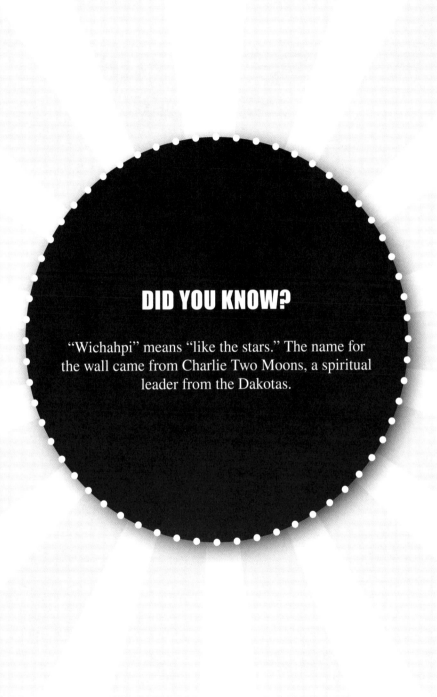

## DID YOU KNOW?

"Wichahpi" means "like the stars." The name for the wall came from Charlie Two Moons, a spiritual leader from the Dakotas.

# GANDER AT GATORS
## AT ALLIGATOR ALLEY

The spring-fed, cypress-filled swamp of Alligator Alley is reminiscent of prehistoric times, so it makes sense that hundreds of prehistoric animals find it a cozy place to call home. Owner Wes Moore captures alligators from unsafe settings, such as golf courses, and relocates them to his alligator attraction, which opened to the public in 2004. More than 450 alligators, ranging from hatchlings to adults, inhabit the land and streams, and as any good owner would, Wes has given them such names as Captain Crunch, Big Moe, and Pickles. At fourteen feet in length, Colonel is the largest gator on the premises.

Trepidatious visitors can stick to strolling along the elevated boardwalk that winds through the swamp, which is also home to less intimidating creatures, such as turtles, ospreys, owls, and bullfrogs, but adventure-seekers can grab some chum and feed the ravenous reptiles, while supervised, of course. For close encounters that aren't quite so hair-raising, head to the Gator Station, where the baby gators live. They love to be held.

19950 Hwy. 71, Summerdale, AL 36580
(251) 946-2483, GatorAlleyFarm.com

# GET MOONED
## BY THE VULCAN

Driving south on Interstate 65, you can't miss seeing this bearded mammoth of a man, and if you head to the Vulcan Park and Museum, you can't help but notice this fella has some pretty nice buns of steel. Or, more correctly, buns of iron.

The fifty-six-foot-tall Vulcan statue sits atop Birmingham's Red Mountain, welcoming visitors to the "Pittsburgh of the South." He's the world's largest cast-iron statue and was created in 1904 to advertise Birmingham's steel and iron industries during the World's Fair in St. Louis. City leaders chose Vulcan because he was the Roman god of fire and forge.

Sculptor Giuseppe Moretti equipped Vulcan with a spear, hammer, and anvil, but Vulcan's apron covers only his front, leaving his posterior exposed. So no matter the day, there's always a full moon over Birmingham.

1701 Valley View Dr., Birmingham, AL 35209
(205) 933-1409, VisitVulcan.com

# MAKE METAL ART
## AT SLOSS FURNACES

Sloss Furnaces sits as a silent monster near Birmingham's city center. Iron ore built this city in the 1870s as blue-collar workers streamed in to take jobs at mines and factories. What's now known as Sloss Furnaces opened as City Furnaces in 1881 and grew into the world's largest manufacturer of crude iron, better known as pig iron.

By the 1970s, demand for domestic iron had decreased dramatically, and Sloss Furnaces shut down production. The facility was revived in the 1980s when it was designated a National Historic Landmark. The site's sprawling campus includes a museum to the city's rich industrial heritage, with two massive four-hundred-ton blast furnaces and around forty other buildings. It is now a unique entertainment venue, and visitors can enjoy concerts on the grounds or participate in metal arts workshops, ranging from blacksmithing and casting to welding and sculpting. Every fall the grounds are turned into a spooky setting for Sloss Fright Furnaces, a haunted attraction.

20 Thirty-Second St. N., Birmingham, AL 35222
(205) 254-2025, SlossFurnaces.com

# PERUSE THE DEALERSHIP
## AT WELLBORN MUSCLECAR MUSEUM

The Wellborn Musclecar Museum celebrates the golden age of American automotive manufacturing with a stunning selection of US-made motor power from the 1960s and '70s. The colorful cars with glistening chrome are displayed showroom-style in an old, renovated dealership in Alexander City.

Owner Tim Wellborn rotates his inventory of road-ready Chargers, Mustangs, and Roadrunners regularly. Of particular interest are the hand-built 1971 Chrysler pilot car and the last ever Hemi Charger built. The collection boasts Hollywood connections with one of the cars actor James Garner drove in *The Rockford Files* and a replica of the famous Trans Am driven by Burt Reynolds in *Smokey and the Bandit*. Your visit to the museum is sure to get you amped up with daydreams of sliding behind the wheel and orchestrating a high-speed getaway from Sheriff Buford T. Justice himself.

124 Broad St., Alexander City, AL 35010
(256) 329-8474, WellbornMusclecarMuseum.com

# MARVEL AT MARBLE STATUES
## IN SYLACAUGA

A vein of pure white marble that runs more than thirty miles and cuts through the city of Sylacauga was discovered in 1820. For more than a century, the rock was highly prized for structural use. It adorns the skylight of the Lincoln Memorial, the inside of the US Supreme Court building, and the outside of the Dime Savings Bank in Brooklyn.

In the 1970s, Sylacauga marble was nearly lost to artists and architects as marble's greatest uses shifted to industrial and pharmaceutical purposes. In 2009, however, citizens worked to recapture the rock's aesthetic value with the first Magic of Marble Festival. Since then, the city's resident sculptor, Craigger Browne, has created and installed pieces around town, including *Once Upon A Time* at the B. B. Comer Memorial Library and *Sylacauga Emerging* at City Hall.

To pick up your own piece of Sylacauga marble, stop by the library, which houses a collection of marble sculptures created by artists during the annual festival.

B. B. Comer Memorial Library
314 N. Broadway Ave., Sylacauga, AL 35150
(256) 249-0961, BBComerLibrary.net/marblefestival

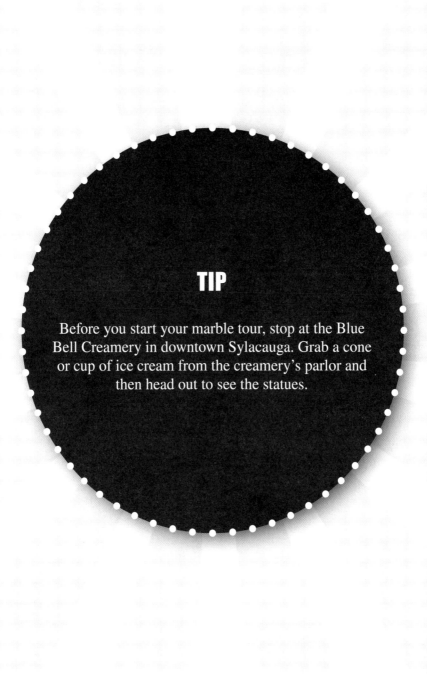

# TIP

Before you start your marble tour, stop at the Blue Bell Creamery in downtown Sylacauga. Grab a cone or cup of ice cream from the creamery's parlor and then head out to see the statues.

# SAY A PRAYER
## AT THE SHRINE OF THE
## MOST BLESSED SACRAMENT

What do you get when an Italian-American nun from Ohio moves to the heart of the Bible Belt? It might sound like the beginning of a corny joke, but in reality you get one of the most stunning shrines in the country. The Shrine of the Most Blessed Sacrament was the fulfillment of Mother Angelica's vision to build a temple for God.

The winding road leading to the shrine takes you through a picturesque pastoral setting of lush green fields and pristine white fences surrounded by rolling hills. The imposing Italian architecture of the piazza and shrine would make St. Francis of Assisi feel at home, and then there's the interior of the shrine with its marble floors and an ornate, handcrafted, gold leaf reredo, or screen.

People of all faiths are welcome at the shrine, and if you listen closely, you may hear David playing his secret chord to please the Lord.

3224 County Rd. 548, Hanceville, AL 35077
(256) 352-6267, olamshrine.com

# SUGGESTED ITINERARIES

## NEAR THE COAST

## AROUND THE BIG CITY OF BIRMINGHAM

• • • • • • • • • • • • • • • • • • • • • • • • • • • •

## IN THE CAPITAL CITY

## AROUND THE WIREGRASS IN SOUTHEAST ALABAMA

• • • • • • • • • • • • • • • • • • • • • • • •

# UP IN THE MOUNTAINS IN NORTHEAST ALABAMA

# SURROUNDING THE SHOALS IN NORTHWEST ALABAMA

• • • • • • • • • • • • • • • • • • • • • • •

# THE BLACK BELT

# AROUND THE ROCKET CITY OF HUNTSVILLE

• • • • • • • • • • • • • • • • • • • • • • • • • • • •

## MILITARY HISTORY

## TAKE A HIKE

• • • • • • • • • • • • • • • • • • • • • • • • •

# FOR ART LOVERS

# FOR SPORTS LOVERS

# FOR HISTORY BUFFS

• • • • • • • • • • • • • • • • • • • • • • • •

Photo courtesy Matt Wilson

# ACTIVITIES BY SEASON

## SPRING

Go on a Pilgrimage to Antebellum Homes (Selma or Eufaula), 110

Smell the Roses and Other Flowers at Bellingrath Gardens, 71

Wade into the Water Surrounded by Cahaba Lilies, 78

Cheer on the Biscuits and Take Home a Hat, 54

Search for Glowing Creatures at Dismals Canyon, 62

Experience the Courtroom Drama *To Kill a Mockingbird* in Monroeville, 26

See the Shrimp Boats during the Blessing of the Fleet in Bayou La Batre, 39

Take in a Race at Barber Motorsports, 63

Celebrate the Music of Hank Williams, 46

Sip Tea with Martha Washington (Festival of Tulips at American Village), 117

## SUMMER

Hike to the Furnaces at Tannehill Ironworks, 114

Enjoy the Scenery and the Spread at Rattlesnake Saloon, 12

Sip Tea with Martha Washington (Independence Day at American Village), 117

Pick a Peach in Chilton County, 19

• • • • • • • • • • • • • • • • • • • • • • • • • •

## FALL

• • • • • • • • • • • • • • • • • • • • • • • • • • • • • • •

# WINTER

• • • • • • • • • • • • • • • • • • • • • • •

Photo courtesy Caleb Hicks

# INDEX

• • • • • • • • • • • • • • • • • • • • • • • • •